The Perfect Words for Every Special Occasion

100+ Messages and Quotes to Help You Celebrate: Birthdays, Weddings, ANNIVERSARY, Birth, NEW HOME, GRADUATION, RETIREMENT, SPECIAL HOLIDAY, and many more.

EMMA TAYLOR

DISCLAIMER!

The contents of the book "**The Perfect Words For Every Special Occasion**," including, but not limited to, the text, graphics, images, and other material contained within, are the exclusive property of the author and are protected under international copyright laws.

Table of Contents

INTRODUCTION

I n a world where communication has become increasingly digital and instantaneous, expressing oneself with the right words for every occasion remains invaluable. The power of thoughtful messages and eloquent quotes extends far beyond mere words on a page; it is a gateway to deeper connections, a tool for navigating life's myriad emotions, and a source of inspiration in times of joy or solace. In the pages of "The Perfect Words For Every Special Occasion," we embark on a journey through the eloquence of language, exploring the myriad ways in which carefully chosen words can transform ordinary moments into extraordinary memories.

Authored by wordsmiths who understand the potency of language, this book is not just a compilation of phrases but a curated collection of sentiments that resonate with the human experience. Whether you celebrate life's joyous milestones, offer solace during times of grief, express love and affection, or seek motivation in the face of challenges, this guide serves as a compass, directing you to the perfect words for each unique circumstance.

"The Perfect Words For Every Special Occasion" is more than a mere reference book; it is a companion on life's journey, a trusted advisor for those moments when words elude us. It is a testament to the belief that meaningful communication remains an art form worth cultivating in a world filled with noise. Through carefully categorized sections, readers can navigate the nuances of various occasions, from birthdays and weddings to sympathy and encouragement, finding just the right words to articulate their thoughts and emotions.

This book does not just provide a reservoir of words; it encourages reflection on the power of language to shape our interactions and influence our relationships. In a time where communication is often reduced to abbreviated text messages and emojis, "The Perfect Words For Every Special Occasion" is a refreshing reminder that language is a multifaceted tool capable of conveying depth, sincerity, and understanding.

Crafting Original and Genuine Messages

Creating an original and genuine wish involves tapping into your sincerity, considering the recipient's personality and the occasion. Here's a step-by-step guide to help you craft such a wish:

Know Your Recipient

Understanding the recipient is foundational to creating a meaningful wish. Consider their personality, preferences, and the context of the occasion. Are they people who appreciate humor, or do they prefer more sentimental messages? What are their interests, and what does the occasion mean to them? The more you know about the recipient, the better you can tailor your wish to resonate with them on a personal level.

Example: If your friend is a nature enthusiast, you might incorporate references to the outdoors or use metaphors related to nature in your wish.

Start with Warmth

The opening sets the tone for your wish. Begin with a warm and genuine greeting that reflects your relationship with the person. Whether it's a simple "Dear [Name]," or a more personalized salutation, the opening should convey your positive feelings and set the stage for the heartfelt message that follows.

Example: "Dear [Friend's Name], Wishing you a day as bright and beautiful as your smile..."

Be Specific and Personal

The heart of an original wish lies in its specificity. Incorporate details unique to the recipient, such as shared memories, inside jokes, or characteristics you admire about them. Personalization shows that you've put thought into the wish, making it more meaningful and memorable.

Example: "Reflecting on the time we [shared a memorable experience], I can't help but appreciate your [unique quality]. Your [attribute] has always made you stand out in the best way, and I hope it continues to shine brightly in the coming year."

Express Genuine Emotion

When expressing genuine emotion in your wish, delve into your specific feelings for the recipient. Instead of using generic phrases, share personal anecdotes or memories that evoke the emotions you want to convey. For example, if you're expressing love, recount a moment that epitomizes that sentiment. If it's pride, highlight a specific achievement or quality that makes you proud. Authenticity shines through when your words are grounded in real, heartfelt experiences.

Example: "As I reflect on our journey together, I can't help but feel an overwhelming sense of gratitude. Your unwavering support during [specific event] and the way you always put others first are just a few reasons why I'm fortunate to have you in my life. Happy [occasion], and here's to many more moments that warm our hearts."

Use Your Own Words

Originality is crucial in crafting a unique wish. Steer clear of clichés or commonly used phrases, and instead, draw from your own vocabulary and experiences. Think about the recipient's personality and your relationship with them. Consider how you would naturally express your feelings in a conversation and translate that into your written wish. This authenticity will make your message stand out and feel more personal.

Example: "On this special day, I wanted to take a moment to tell you how much your resilience and kindness inspire me. Your ability to find joy in the little things and spread positivity is truly remarkable. Here's to celebrating the wonderful person you are and your incredible impact on those around you."

Be Positive and Uplifting

Opt for a positive and uplifting tone in your wish, especially when celebrating joyous occasions. Highlight the person's positive qualities or focus on the optimistic aspects of the moment. Share your hopes for their continued success, happiness, or fulfillment. By infusing positivity into your wish, you contribute to creating a joyful atmosphere that aligns with the celebratory nature of the occasion.

Example: "Happy Anniversary! As we reflect on the beautiful journey of the past [number] years, I am filled with gratitude for the love, laughter, and countless memories we've shared. Here's to the next chapter of our adventure, where I look forward to creating even more cherished moments and navigating life's joys together. To us and the endless possibilities ahead!"

Include a Personal Touch

Adding a personal touch to your wish helps make it uniquely yours. Consider the recipient's interests, hobbies, or shared experiences. Reference a moment that holds sentimental value between you and the person. This personal touch reinforces the authenticity of your message, showing that you've taken the time to make it special.

Example: "Happy Anniversary! Just like our favorite [shared interest], may your relationship continue to blossom and bring you as much joy as our [memorable experience]."

Look to the Future

Expressing hope and excitement for the future adds a forward-looking perspective to your wish. Whether it's for a birthday, a new job, or any milestone, expressing optimism for what lies ahead can be uplifting. This also helps the recipient anticipate positive experiences and creates a sense of anticipation.

Example: "Congratulations on your new job! May this opportunity open doors to even greater success and fulfillment in the days to come. Here's to the exciting journey that lies ahead!"

Keep It Concise

While providing details is essential, keeping your wish concise is equally important. A succinct message ensures that your main sentiments are clear and impactful. Long messages might risk losing the recipient's attention or diluting the emotional impact. Aim for clarity, choosing words that capture the essence of your wish without unnecessary elaboration.

Example: "Happy Graduation! Your hard work and dedication have paid off, and I have no doubt that your future is destined for greatness. Cheers to your achievements and the exciting road that lies ahead!"

Remember, each of these elements contributes to the overall authenticity and uniqueness of your wish. Balancing personalization, positivity, and conciseness ensures that your message resonates with the recipient meaningfully.

As we delve into the pages of this guide, we embark on a quest for eloquence, armed with the knowledge that the right words have the potential to heal wounds, strengthen bonds, and celebrate the richness of the human experience. So, whether you are a seasoned wordsmith or someone exploring the art of expression, join us on this literary voyage through the landscapes of emotion, where the right words await discovery for every occasion life presents.

BIRTHDAYS

Birthdays are special times when we get to show our friends and loved ones how much they mean to us. But with all the texting and social media, it's easy to fall into the habit of sending quick, generic messages. This chapter is here to help you bring back the personal touch in your birthday greetings. It's like a friendly helper, giving you tips and ideas to create heartfelt and memorable messages for the people you care about.

Birthdays are more than just a date on the calendar; they're a chance to connect with others and spread joy. Whether you're good with words or struggle to find the right ones, this guide is filled with inspiration and practical advice to make your birthday messages stand out. Whether you're writing a card or sending a digital message, it doesn't matter – this guide has something for everyone.

In today's world, where we're all connected online, this book understands the need to adapt traditional sentiments to fit how we communicate. From sweet handwritten notes to clever digital messages, you will see how to make your greetings special and tailored to each person. You'll learn how to add genuine feelings, match your words to someone's personality, and even bring in shared memories.

Through stories, examples, and easy exercises, this guide helps you understand the ins and outs of expressing warmth and sincerity in your birthday messages. It discusses why personalizing your message is important, how your tone can make a big difference, and the simple art of including memories in your wishes. Whether you're writing to a friend, family member, coworker, or someone special, this book gives you the tools to create messages that reflect your unique relationship.

It isn't just a guide to writing birthday messages – it's a journey into the power of words to connect and build relationships. As you flip through these pages, may you find ideas, tips, and the confidence to turn your birthday messages into meaningful expressions of love and celebration.

General Birthday Wishes

Birthdays, the common thread that unites us all, call for expressions of joy that transcend specific bonds. Whether you're writing to someone you've known for years or extending warm wishes to a new acquaintance, the sentiments within "General Birthday Wishes" are designed to strike the perfect balance of warmth, positivity, and genuine celebration.

In this section, we delve into the art of creating birthday messages that are inclusive and adaptable, ensuring that your words resonate with a broad audience. From cheerful and lighthearted greetings to thoughtful and reflective sentiments, you'll find a spectrum of ideas that cater to various personalities and relationships. Whether you're aiming for simplicity, elegance, or a touch of humor, "General Birthday Wishes" provides the foundation for crafting messages that leave a lasting impression.

So, without further ado, let's explore the enchanting world of "General Birthday Wishes" and discover the art of sending universal messages that make every birthday a truly special occasion.

Messages

V1. *Classic Birthday Greeting* (#001)

"Happy Birthday! On this special day, may joy wrap you in its warm embrace, laughter fill your surroundings, and your heart overflow with love. May the year ahead be a canvas of beautiful moments, painted with happiness and sprinkled with success. Cheers to another year of wonderful adventures!"

V2. *Warm and Heartfelt Wish for a Friend* (#002)

"To an incredible friend on their special day – Happy Birthday! Your presence adds a magical touch to life, and I'm grateful for the laughter, shared memories, and countless moments we've experienced together. May your day be as amazing as you are, and may the year ahead bring you all the happiness you deserve."

V3. *Sincere Birthday Message for Family* (#003)

"Wishing the most wonderful [brother/sister/mom/dad] a very Happy Birthday! Your love and guidance are the pillars of our family, and today is all about celebrating you. May this year be filled with health, happiness, and the fulfillment of all your dreams. Here's to creating more cherished memories together!"

V4. *Funny Birthday Greeting* (#004)

"Happy Birthday! You know you're getting old when the candles cost more than the cake. But age is just a number, right? May your day be filled with surprises, laughter, and maybe a few less wrinkles than last year. Cheers to embracing the wisdom that comes with each passing year!"

V5. Birthday Wish for a Colleague (#005)

"Warmest birthday wishes to an exceptional colleague! Your dedication and positive spirit make the workplace brighter for everyone. May this special day be a break from spreadsheets and meetings, filled with joy, relaxation, and a well-deserved celebration. Here's to another year of professional achievements and personal growth!"

V6. Encouraging Birthday Message (#006)

"Happy Birthday! Another year, another opportunity for growth and new beginnings. May this chapter bring you the courage to chase your dreams, the strength to overcome challenges, and the wisdom to savor life's precious moments. Wishing you a year ahead filled with personal triumphs and joyous milestones!"

V7. Thoughtful Birthday Wish for a Loved One (#007)

"On your special day, I want you to know how much you mean to me. Happy Birthday! Your kindness, warmth, and love light up my world. May this year be a reflection of the joy you bring into the lives of others. Here's to celebrating you and the beautiful soul you are!"

V8. Birthday Blessings for a Religious Friend (#008)

"Happy Birthday! On this special day, may the divine light shine upon you, filling your life with love, peace, and boundless blessings. May your journey be guided by faith, and may you find strength in the embrace of those who cherish and support you. Wishing you a year of spiritual growth and fulfillment."

V9. Adventurous Birthday Wish (#009)

"Happy Birthday, adventurer! May your year ahead be as thrilling as scaling new heights and as full of surprises as exploring uncharted territories. Here's to embracing challenges, seizing opportunities, and creating memories that will last a lifetime. May your journey be as exciting as the destination!"

V10. Poetic Birthday Greeting (#010)

"As the sun rises on this day, so does a celebration of you. Happy Birthday! May your life be a symphony of laughter, your dreams dance with the stars, and your heart be a canvas painted with vibrant hues of joy. May each passing year be a melody of love and fulfillment. Cheers to your unique and beautiful journey!"

Milestone Birthdays

There's something uniquely special about reaching those pivotal moments known as milestone birthdays. These numerical signposts prompt reflection, celebration, and often a bit of introspection. From the exciting transition to double digits to the reflective journey into the golden years, milestone birthdays offer an opportunity to pause and appreciate the journey thus far while looking forward to the adventures ahead. In exploring milestone birthdays, we delve into the significance of these special occasions and how they shape our lives.

The journey through life is a series of milestones, and birthdays serve as checkpoints that remind us of the distance traveled. From the exuberant Sweet Sixteen to the reflective Fifty, each milestone birthday carries its own unique weight and significance. These moments provide an opportunity for individuals to take stock of their experiences, accomplishments, and dreams, creating a sense of continuity and purpose in the grand narrative of life.

As we navigate the chapters of our lives, milestone birthdays become a canvas upon which we paint the colors of our memories, lessons learned, and goals yet to be achieved. They prompt us to celebrate the triumphs, embrace the challenges, and appreciate the beauty of the journey. Whether it's the symbolic "coming of age" at 18, the wisdom accompanying 30, or the esteemed jubilation of turning 100, each milestone offers a chance to reflect on the unique blend of joy and growth that defines our individual stories.

Moreover, milestone birthdays are not just personal celebrations; they are occasions that bring communities together. Friends, family, and loved ones join in marking these significant moments, expressing gratitude, and showering the individual with well-wishes and affection. It's a time for shared laughter, tears, and hopes for the future. So, join us as we celebrate life, one milestone birthday at a time.

Legal Eighteen: Unlocking Adulthood

The eighteenth birthday is a legal milestone, signifying the transition to adulthood. It marks the moment when individuals gain the right to vote, serve on juries, and make their own decisions regarding important life choices. It's a celebration of newfound responsibilities and the beginning of a journey into the complexities of the adult world.

Messages

V1. Message of Encouragement (#011)

Happy Sweet Sixteen! As you step into this incredible chapter of your life, I want you to embrace the newfound independence that comes with being sixteen. This is a time for self-discovery, adventure, and learning. May you navigate the path ahead with courage and curiosity, and may every moment be a stepping stone toward the amazing person you are destined to become. Wishing you a year filled with laughter, growth, and unforgettable experiences. Happy birthday!

V2. Parental Reflection (#012)

To our incredible daughter on her Sweet Sixteen, where has the time gone? It feels like you were taking your first steps just yesterday, and now you're stepping into a world of independence. We are so proud of the beautiful soul you've become. As you embrace this new chapter, know that our love and support are unwavering. May your journey be filled with joy, self-discovery, and the fulfillment of your dreams. Happy Sweet Sixteen, sweetheart.

V3. Friendship and Adventure (#013)

Cheers to sixteen years of laughter, shared secrets, and countless adventures! Happy Sweet Sixteen, my dear friend! As we stand at the threshold of independence, I can't wait to see all the amazing experiences and memories that await us. May this year be filled with exciting escapades, personal triumphs, and the continued growth of our unbreakable bond. Here's to embracing independence and celebrating the incredible journey ahead.

V4. Mentor's Words of Wisdom (#014)

Happy Sweet Sixteen to an extraordinary young person! As you embark on this journey of independence, remember that true strength lies in authenticity and self-discovery. Embrace the challenges, relish the victories, and don't forget to learn from every experience. Your potential is limitless, and I can't wait to see your incredible impact on the world. Wishing you a year filled with growth, wisdom, and the courage to be uniquely you.

V5. Sibling's Heartfelt Wishes (#015)

To my not-so-little sibling, Happy Sweet Sixteen! It's amazing to see you growing up into such an incredible person. As you embrace this newfound independence, remember you have a sibling who is always here for you. May this year bring you exciting adventures, self-discovery, and the realization of your dreams. You're not just a year older but a step closer to becoming the amazing person you are meant to be. Happy birthday, and here's to many more shared moments on this journey called life.

Twenty-One: Toasting to Freedom

In many cultures, the twenty-first birthday is synonymous with reaching the legal drinking age. Beyond the festivities, it symbolizes a rite of passage, marking the entrance into a world of increased privileges, responsibilities, and the freedom to make one's own choices.

Messages

V1. Reflective Rhapsody on Turning Twenty-One (#016)

As you stand on the cusp of twenty-one, let us take a moment to reflect on the incredible journey that has led you to this milestone. Your laughter, tears, triumphs, and challenges have all shaped the remarkable person you've become. As you raise your glass to toast to freedom, remember that this newfound age is not just about legal privileges but a celebration of the autonomy to shape your own narrative. May this year be filled with adventures, self-discovery, and the sweet taste of the freedom you so rightly deserve.

V2. A Toast to the Threshold of Adulthood (#017)

Here's to you stepping boldly into the realm of adulthood! As you turn twenty-one, it's not just about legal libations; it's a symbolic journey into a world of profound responsibilities and exhilarating possibilities. May this year be a canvas for you to paint your dreams and ambitions with vibrant hues. Embrace the challenges, relish the victories, and savor the joy of navigating life's twists and turns. Here's to the adventures that await and the remarkable adult you are destined to become.

V3. *Liberation and Libations: Cheers to Twenty-One!* (#018)

Raise your glass high and let the clink of it against others be the anthem of your liberation. Turning twenty-one isn't just about being of legal age; it's about embracing the freedom to carve your own path, make your own choices, and revel in the uniqueness that defines you. As you embark on this journey, may every sip of success be sweet, every stumble be a lesson, and every celebration echo with the resounding cheers of a life lived authentically.

V4. *A Symphony of Twenty-One Years* (#019)

Imagine life as a grand symphony, and at twenty-one; you are about to compose a movement uniquely yours. Each note represents a memory, every crescendo a triumph, and the pauses, the spaces where you've learned and grown. As you step onto the stage of twenty-one, may your symphony be filled with harmonious moments, bold choices, and the sweet melody of freedom? Cheers to orchestrating a life that resonates with the music of your heart.

V5. *The Key to the Kingdom of Twenty-One* (#020)

Twenty-one is the age when the key to the kingdom of adulthood is finally in your hands. Unlock the doors to new experiences, open the gates to self-discovery, and walk the path toward your dreams. May this year be a tapestry woven with threads of independence, resilience, and the joy of navigating life on your terms. Here's to the adventures that await, the lessons that will shape you, and the freedom that is now yours to savor and relish. Cheers to twenty-one, where every toast is a celebration of the extraordinary journey you're embarking upon!

The Big Three-Oh: Reflection and Renewal

Turning thirty often prompts introspection and reflection on personal and professional achievements. It's a milestone where individuals may reevaluate goals, relationships, and priorities. The thirtieth birthday can be seen as an opportunity for self-renewal and the embrace of a more mature and focused chapter of life.

Messages

V1. Embracing the Thirties: A Journey of Reflection and Renewal (#021)

As you stand at the threshold of the Big Three-Oh, take a moment to reflect on the incredible journey that has brought you to this milestone. Your twenties were a whirlwind of self-discovery, challenges, and triumphs. As you step into this new chapter, embrace the opportunity for renewal. Let go of what no longer serves you, and welcome the wisdom that comes with a decade of experience. May your thirties be a canvas where you paint the masterpiece of your life, filled with purpose, growth, and the joy of becoming the person you were meant to be.

V2. Thirty and Thriving: A Chapter Unfolding (#022)

Happy 30th birthday! Today marks the beginning of a chapter filled with possibilities, growth, and a deep sense of self-awareness. Your twenties were events of lessons, shaping you into the resilient, incredible individual you are now. As you celebrate this milestone, take a moment to reflect on your journey – the challenges conquered, the dreams pursued, and the friendships that have stood the test of time. May your thirties be a period of thriving, where you continue to explore, learn, and flourish in the rich soil of experience.

V3. *Cheers to Thirty: Navigating the Next Decade* (#023)

Here's to thirty incredible years of life, love, and laughter! As you embark on the next leg of your journey, consider this milestone not a destination but a launchpad into a new era of self-discovery and purpose. Reflect on the lessons of the past and let them guide you toward a future filled with intention and authenticity. May your thirties be a time of navigating life's twists and turns with grace, courage, and the unwavering belief that the best is yet to come.

V4. *A Decade Unveiled: Unwrapping the Gift of Thirty* (#024)

Happy 30th! Today, unwrap the gift of a new decade, adorned with the ribbons of experience and tied with the bows of memories. Your journey so far has sculpted you into a unique masterpiece, and now, as you stand on the cusp of thirty, embrace the unfolding of a new chapter. Take this moment to reflect on the resilience you've shown, the dreams you've chased, and the love you've shared. May your thirties be a canvas where you paint the vibrant strokes of your aspirations, creating a masterpiece reflecting your true self's essence.

V5. *Entering the Third Decade: A Symphony of Growth* (#025)

Happy 30th birthday! As you step into the third decade of your life, let the symphony of growth and self-discovery play on. Your twenties were the overture, setting the stage for the intricate composition ahead. Reflect on the melodies of joy, the harmonies of challenges, and the crescendos of triumphs that have shaped you. Now, with each note, create a future filled with purpose, authenticity, and the resounding beauty of embracing the journey of becoming. May your thirties be a symphony of your most authentic self, resonating with the rhythm of a life well-lived.

Half a Century: The Golden Fifty

Reaching the age of fifty is a golden milestone, symbolizing a wealth of life experiences and the wisdom that comes with it. It's an opportune time for reflection, gratitude, and a celebration of the enduring resilience that has carried individuals through five decades of existence.

Messages

V1. Reflective Journey at Fifty: A Golden Milestone (#026)

As you stand at the threshold of fifty, it's a moment to pause and reflect on the incredible journey that has brought you to this golden milestone. This is not just a celebration of the passage of time; it's a testament to the myriad experiences, lessons learned, and triumphs achieved. May this milestone bridge the cherished memories of the past and the boundless possibilities of the future. Happy 50th birthday, marking not just the halfway point but the golden culmination of a life well-lived.

V2. The Golden Tapestry of Fifty Years (#027)

Fifty years—a period that weaves a golden shade of moments, each thread representing laughter, tears, victories, and resilience. Your fiftieth birthday is not just an occasion to mark the passing of time but an opportunity to marvel at the intricacies of this tapestry. Each stitch is a story, and as you celebrate this milestone, may you bask in the warmth of the golden glow that emanates from a life richly lived. Happy 50th birthday, a celebration of the masterpiece that is you.

V3. Navigating the Rivers of Fifty: A Journey Well-Traveled (#028)

Like a seasoned navigator, you've charted the rivers of life for fifty years, steering through the twists and turns with grace and determination. This milestone birthday is a tribute to the journey—the calm waters, the turbulent rapids, and the serene lakes you've encountered. As you stand at the helm of fifty, may the winds of joy fill your sails, carrying you into the next half-century with renewed vigor and the promise of even more extraordinary adventures. Happy 50th birthday, captain of your destiny.

V4. A Symphony of Fifty: Notes of Resilience and Harmony (#029)

Fifty years, much like a symphony, composed of varied notes—some soft, others bold; moments of joy blending with echoes of challenges. Your fiftieth birthday celebrates the unique melody you've crafted, filled with the richness of experiences and the harmonious blend of highs and lows. May the next movement of your life's symphony be as grand and fulfilling as the first fifty years have been. Happy birthday to the conductor of a beautiful life composition.

V5. Fifty and Flourishing: A Garden of Achievements (#030)

Imagine your life as a flourishing garden and, each year, a new bloom of accomplishment. As you reach the fiftieth bloom, take a moment to stroll through the garden of your journey—the vibrant colors of achievements, the sturdy stems of resilience, and the fragrant blossoms of love and laughter. Happy 50th birthday, a celebration not just of the individual blooms but of the entire magnificent garden that is your life. May the next fifty years bring even more blossoms of joy and fulfillment.

Retirement Seventy: A New Beginning

The seventieth birthday often aligns with the beginning of retirement for many individuals. It's a milestone that signifies the culmination of a dedicated working life and the commencement of a new chapter filled with leisure, exploration, and the pursuit of personal passions.

Messages

V1. Reflecting on a Lifetime of Achievement (#031)

As you step into seventy, take a moment to reflect on the incredible journey that has brought you to this point. Your seven decades have been filled with dedication, hard work, and a commitment to excellence. May this new chapter of retirement be a time for you to relish in the accomplishments of your career, savor the memories you've created, and embrace the endless possibilities that lie ahead.

V2. A Toast to Seventy and a Life Well-Lived (#032)

Here's to you on your seventieth birthday, a day that marks the passing of another year and the beginning of a new and exciting chapter—retirement. Your dedication to your work has inspired us all, and now it's time for you to enjoy the fruits of your labor. May this new beginning be filled with relaxation, adventure, and the joy of pursuing the passions that may have taken a back seat during your working years.

V3. Wishing You a Retirement of Blissful Freedom (#033)

Happy seventieth birthday! As you embark on this retirement journey, may you find the blissful freedom that comes with stepping away from the demands of the workplace. May your days be filled with leisurely pursuits, moments of serenity, and the pursuit of all the dreams and desires you've harbored over the years. Here's to a new beginning where each day unfolds at your own pace, a pace dictated solely by your heart's desires.

V4. Seventy and Still Soaring: The Adventure Continues (#034)

Celebrating seven decades of life is a remarkable feat, and now, as you transition into retirement, the adventure continues. May your seventieth birthday be a launchpad for new experiences, unexplored passions, and the thrill of discovering the richness of life beyond the confines of the workplace. May your retirement be a canvas waiting for the vibrant strokes of your dreams and desires.

V5. *Embracing the Blank Canvas of Retirement* (#035)

As you enter the realm of retirement, envision it as a blank canvas awaiting the brush strokes of your newfound freedom. May your seventieth birthday mark not only the passage of time but the beginning of a new chapter where you paint the canvas of your life with the colors of joy, relaxation, and the pursuit of all that brings fulfillment to your heart. Cheers to a retirement filled with endless possibilities and a canvas awaiting your unique masterpiece.

Birthday Quotes from Notable Figures

- "And in the end, it's not the years in your life that count. It's the life in your years." - **Abraham Lincoln.**

- "Age is whatever you think it is. You are as old as you think you are." - **Muhammad Ali.**

- "If we could be twice young and twice old, we could correct all our mistakes." - **Euripides.**

- "Age is a case of mind over matter. If you don't mind, it doesn't matter." - **Satchel Paige.**

- "The great thing about getting older is that you don't lose all the other ages you've been." - **Madeleine L'Engle.**

- "May you live as long as you want and never want as long as you live." - **Irish Blessing**

- "The more you praise and celebrate your life, the more there is in life to celebrate." - **Oprah Winfrey.**

- "With mirth and laughter, let old wrinkles come." - **William Shakespeare**

- "The secret of staying young is to live honestly, eat slowly, and lie about your age." - **Lucille Ball**

- "It takes a long time to become young." - **Pablo Picasso**

- "Every birthday is a gift. Every day is a gift." - **Aretha Franklin**

- "No wise man ever wished to be younger." - **Jonathan Swift**

- "May you live to be 100, and may the last voice you hear be mine." - **Frank Sinatra**

- "You know you're getting old when the candles cost more than the cake." - **Bob Hope**

- "A birthday is just another day where you go to work and people give you love. Age is just a state of mind, and you are as old as you think you are. You have to count your blessings and be happy." - **Abhishek Bachchan**

- "Just remember, once you're over the hill you begin to pick up speed." - **Charles Schulz.**

- "The best birthdays of all are those that haven't arrived yet." - **Robert Orben.**

- "Live not one's life as though one had a thousand years, but live each day as the last." - **Marcus Aurelius**

- "All the world is birthday cake, so take a piece, but not too much." - **George Harrison.**

- "Youth is happy because it has the ability to see beauty. Anyone who keeps the ability to see beauty never grows old." - **Franz Kafka**

- "Age is strictly a case of mind over matter. If you don't mind, it doesn't matter." - **Jack Benny.**

WEDDINGS

A wedding is a ceremony that unites two people in marriage. Wedding traditions and customs differ significantly between cultures, ethnic groups, races, faiths, denominations, countries, socioeconomic backgrounds, and sexual orientations. Most wedding rituals include the exchange of marital vows by the couple, providing a gift (offering rings, symbolic items, flowers, money, or a dress), and a public declaration of marriage by an authority figure or celebrant. Special wedding attire is frequently worn, and a wedding celebration occasionally follows the service. As are superstitious customs, music, poetry, prayers, or readings from religious books or literature are all common elements of the ritual.

Many nations have inherited the classic Western custom of the white wedding, which involves the bride wearing a white wedding gown and veil. Some civilizations have inherited the classic Western custom of the white wedding, which involves a woman wearing a white wedding gown and veil. This ritual gained popularity following Queen Victoria's marriage. Some argue that Queen Victoria's choice of a white gown was not only extravagant but also influenced by her ideals, which stressed sexual purity.

Wearing a wedding ring has long been an element of religious weddings in Europe and America, but the tradition's origin is unknown. One explanation is the Roman belief in the Vena amoris, which was thought to be a blood vessel that connected the fourth finger (ring finger) directly to the heart. Thus, when a couple wore rings on this finger, their hearts were united. According to historian Vicki Howard, the notion of the "ancient" nature of the activity is most likely a contemporary fabrication. A groom's wedding band was not introduced in the United States until the early twentieth century, but it has been a practice in Europe since the ancient Romans, as evidenced by the jurist Gaius.

The wedding ceremony is frequently followed by a wedding reception or a wedding brunch, during which customs may include speeches by the groom, best man, father of the bride, and possibly the bride, the newlyweds' first dance as a couple, and the cutting of a beautiful wedding cake. In recent years, traditions have evolved to include a father-daughter dance for a bride and her father and a mother-son dance for the groom and his mother.

Guide to Writing Heartfelt Wedding Messages

Weddings are joyous occasions that celebrate the union of two individuals embarking on a lifelong journey together. Crafting the perfect wedding message is a thoughtful and cherished way to convey your love, support, and best wishes to the newlyweds. This guide is designed to help you navigate the art of writing heartfelt wedding messages, whether you're penning a card, a toast, or a social media post.

Choosing the Right Tone

Before crafting your message, take a moment to consider the couple's personalities, interests, and values. Tailoring your words to reflect their unique bond adds a personal touch. Also, maintain a balance between sincerity and lightheartedness. Your message should convey warmth and joy while respecting the formality of the occasion.

Elements of a Wedding Message

Begin your message by extending heartfelt congratulations to the couple. Acknowledge the significance of their commitment and celebrate their love. Then, include shared memories or anecdotes highlighting your connection with the couple, if applicable. This personal touch adds warmth and nostalgia to your message.

You can go ahead by imparting wisdom or advice for a successful marriage, which can be a meaningful addition to your message. Share insights gained from your experiences or offer well-wishes for their journey. Acknowledge the beauty of the wedding ceremony, the venue, or any special moments you observed. Complimenting these details shows attentiveness and genuine appreciation for the day.

Writing Wedding Card Messages

When writing a wedding card, ensure your message is concise yet heartfelt. Space may be limited, so choose your words carefully.

Examples

Formal Message:

Dear [Couple's Names],

Heartfelt congratulations on your wedding day! May your journey together be filled with love, laughter, and endless joy. I wish you a lifetime of happiness.

Warm regards,

[Your Name]

Personalized Message:

Dear [Couple's Names],

As you embark on this beautiful journey together, may your days be filled with the same joy you've brought into each other's lives. Remember that love is not just spoken; it's lived. Congratulations on your special day!

Much love,

[Your Name]

Crafting Wedding Toasts

When giving a wedding toast, start with a warm greeting and express gratitude for being part of the celebration.

Structure

- **Opening:** Express your happiness for the couple.
- **Anecdote or Memory:** Share a brief and relevant story.
- **Message:** Convey your best wishes and offer a toast to their future.

Example: "Good evening, everyone! I stand here with immense joy and honor to toast to the incredible love between [Couple's Names]. From the moment I met them, it was evident that they were destined for something extraordinary..."

[Continue with a personal story and conclude with a toast]

Writing wedding messages is an art that allows you to contribute to the joy of a couple's special day. Understanding the couple, striking the right tone, and incorporating personal touches will make your message a cherished part of their wedding memories. Whether it's a card, a toast, or a social media post, your words have the power to convey love, support, and the warmest of wishes.

Congratulations and Best Wishes

When you offer congratulations on someone's marriage, you're expressing joy and happiness for the couple's union. It's a way of acknowledging and celebrating their commitment to each other. The sentiment goes beyond simply acknowledging the event; it carries the weight of good wishes for their future together. Saying "congratulations" in the context of marriage recognizes the significance of the commitment and the beginning of a new chapter in the couple's life.

Sending best wishes to a newly married couple expresses your hope and desire for their future happiness. It goes beyond celebrating the wedding day itself, extending goodwill for the days, months, and years to come. Best wishes convey a positive outlook and a genuine hope that the couple's journey together will be filled with love, joy, and prosperity. This phrase encapsulates the sentiment that you want nothing but the best for the couple as they embark on their married life.

In summary, "congratulations" acknowledges the achievement of getting married, while "best wishes" extends positive sentiments for the ongoing journey of marital life. These expressions reflect your happiness for the couple's union and your hope for a fulfilling and joyful future together.

Messages

V1. Heartfelt Wishes for a Lifetime of Love (#036)

Congratulations on finding your forever love! May your marriage be a journey filled with laughter, joy, and unwavering companionship. Wishing you both a lifetime of shared dreams, mutual respect, and a love that grows stronger with each passing day.

V2. *Warmest Congratulations on Your Wedding Day* (#037)

As you embark on this beautiful journey together, may your days be filled with love that knows no bounds. May your home be a sanctuary of happiness, understanding, and unwavering support. Congratulations on tying the knot, and here's to a lifetime of shared adventures and cherished moments.

V3. *A Toast to Your Everlasting Love* (#038)

Cheers to the newlyweds! May your marriage be a symphony of laughter, a dance of understanding, and a celebration of each other's uniqueness. Here's to creating a lifetime of memories, overcoming challenges hand in hand, and discovering the true magic of love. Congratulations on your wedding day!

V4. *Wishing You a Fairytale Marriage* (#039)

As you step into this new chapter of your life, may your love story be a modern fairytale filled with passion, commitment, and endless romance. Congratulations on finding your happily ever after! May your days be filled with the warmth of love and the magic of shared dreams.

V5. *Congratulations on Your Union* (#040)

On this joyous occasion, I extend my heartfelt congratulations to both of you. May your marriage be woven with patience, understanding, and boundless love. May the journey ahead be marked by beautiful sunsets, shared laughter, and a love that only deepens with the passage of time.

V6. *Warmest Wishes for Your Marital Bliss* (#041)

I am sending my sincerest congratulations on your wedding day! May your journey as a married couple be sprinkled with love, kindness, and countless moments of joy. May you navigate the seas of life together, weathering storms and basking in the sunshine. Here's to a lifetime of marital bliss!

V7. *May Your Love Story Continue to Blossom* (#042)

Heartiest congratulations on your wedding! May your love story continue to blossom like a beautiful garden, with each passing day bringing new colors and fragrances. May you nurture the seeds of your relationship with care, tenderness, and unwavering commitment.

V8. *Wishing You a Love That Grows Stronger* (#043)

Congratulations on your marriage! May the flame of your love burn eternally bright. May you navigate the twists and turns of life with grace, and may your bond strengthen with every challenge you overcome together. Here's to a love that grows stronger with each passing day.

V9. *Congratulations on Your Nuptials* (#044)

As you stand at the threshold of this new chapter, accept my warmest congratulations on your wedding. May your union be a source of inspiration, laughter, and endless love. May you find comfort in each other's arms and solace in each other's hearts throughout the journey of life.

V10. *A Lifetime of Shared Dreams and Adventures* (#045)

Congratulations on your wedding day! May your marriage be an exciting adventure filled with shared dreams, laughter, and mutual growth. May you both find strength in each other, comfort in your togetherness, and the courage to face whatever comes your way. Here's to a lifetime of love and happiness!

Wedding Anniversary Messages

Wedding anniversary messages are expressions of love, celebration, and reflection shared between spouses to commemorate the special day when they exchanged vows and began their journey together. These messages play a crucial role in celebrating the enduring bond between a married couple, acknowledging the time and experiences they have shared, and expressing hopes for the future.

Here are key elements and considerations when crafting wedding anniversary messages:

- Anniversary messages often include reflections on the journey the couple has taken together. This could involve recalling significant moments, and challenges overcome, and the growth they've experienced as individuals and as a couple.

- Messages are an opportunity to express deep love and gratitude for the partner. Couples often use affectionate words to convey the importance of their spouse in their lives and their appreciation for the love and support received throughout the marriage.

- Acknowledge the achievements and milestones the couple has reached together. This could include personal accomplishments, career successes, or any shared goals realized over the years.

- Wedding anniversary messages frequently include expressions of hope and anticipation for the future. Couples may share aspirations and dreams and reaffirm their commitment to facing life's journey together, hand in hand.

- Depending on the couple's sense of humor, some messages may incorporate playful or humorous elements. A well-placed joke or a lighthearted reference to shared experiences can add warmth and laughter to the celebration.

- Many anniversary messages use poetic or romantic language to evoke emotions and convey the depth of love. Quotes, metaphors, or heartfelt poetry can enhance the sentimental value of the message.

- While anniversaries are often joyful occasions, acknowledging challenges and expressing gratitude for overcoming them can add sincerity and authenticity to the message. It reflects the resilience and strength of the marriage.

In essence, wedding anniversary messages are an opportunity to celebrate love, express gratitude, and reflect on the shared journey of a married couple. Each message is a unique expression of the bond that continues to strengthen with each passing year.

Messages

V1. Celebrating a Love That Grows Stronger: Happy Anniversary! (#046)

As you commemorate another year of love and companionship, may your hearts be filled with the warmth of the memories you've created together. Your journey is an inspiring testament to the power of enduring love, resilience, and the beauty of a relationship that grows stronger each day. Here's to many more years of shared laughter, cherished moments, and a love that only deepens with time.

V2. A Decade of Togetherness: Happy 10th Anniversary! (#047)

A decade of marriage is not just a milestone; it's a creation of dedication, understanding, and unwavering love. Your ten years together stand as a testament to the dedication you've poured into your relationship. May this special day be adorned with joy, reflection, and the anticipation of many more years of shared adventures, growth, and love that will continue to blossom.

I am wishing you a joyous anniversary!

V3. Two Hearts, One Journey: Happy Anniversary to a Beautiful Couple (#048)

On this special day, I celebrate the union of two hearts that embarked on a beautiful journey together. Your love story is a source of inspiration, a reminder that true love knows no bounds. May this anniversary be filled with laughter, moments of reflection, and the reaffirmation of your enduring commitment to one another. Here's to the intertwining of your lives and the magic that happens when two hearts beat as one.

V4. 25 Years of Love and Laughter: Happy Silver Anniversary! (#049)

Congratulations on reaching this remarkable milestone of 25 years of marriage! A silver anniversary is a symbol of enduring love, shared dreams, and countless memories. Your journey together is a shining example of commitment, sacrifice, and the beauty of a love that withstands the tests of time. May this day be a celebration of the incredible bond you've built and a joyful reflection on the countless adventures that lie ahead.

V5. Through Thick and Thin: Happy Anniversary to a Resilient Couple (#050)

As you celebrate another year of marriage, I am reminded of the strength and resilience that defines your relationship. Your commitment to each other has remained unwavering through the highs and lows. May this anniversary be a moment to acknowledge the challenges you've conquered together and the love that has only deepened as a result. Here's to a lifetime of continued growth, unwavering support, and a love that triumphs over all.

Marriage Advice and Well-Wishes

As couples embark on this adventure, they are often greeted with a flood of marriage advice and well-wishes from family, friends, and well-meaning acquaintances. These words of wisdom and heartfelt expressions of goodwill form a pillar of support, providing guidance and encouragement as the newlyweds set sail into the uncharted waters of matrimony.

Marriage advice, often shared with the best intentions, is a compass handed down through generations. It encompasses a spectrum of insights, from the practical to the profound, each piece serving as a nugget of wisdom to navigate the complexities of married life. Advice often centers around communication, compromise, and understanding—the cornerstones of a successful partnership. Elders may counsel patience, reminding couples that storms will come, but with a sturdy vessel built on love and mutual respect, they can weather any storm that arises.

In a world where the landscape of relationships is ever-evolving, advice extends beyond the conventional. Modern well-wishers may emphasize equality, partnership, and the importance of maintaining individual identities within the union. Acknowledging that marriage is a dynamic and reciprocal journey, these contemporary insights encourage couples to grow together while nurturing their individual aspirations and dreams.

Like gentle breezes, well-wishes carry the hopes and blessings of those who have witnessed the union. They are the heartfelt expressions that echo through the corridors of time, affirming the couple's commitment and shared joy. These wishes often encapsulate the essence of enduring love, happiness, and a life filled with shared adventures. Whether conveyed through eloquent prose, simple sentiments, or poetic verses, well-wishes become the affirmations that surround the couple, enveloping them in a cocoon of positive energy.

Marriage advice and well-wishes serve as anchors in times of challenge, grounding couples amidst possible uncertainties. They remind partners of their promises to each other on their wedding day, encouraging them to cherish the bond they have created. These messages' shared experiences and lessons become beacons of hope, guiding couples through the ebb and flow of married life.

However, couples need to recognize that while advice and well-wishes are valuable, each marriage is unique. The key lies in embracing the shared wisdom while allowing room for personal growth and discovery. Just as no two individuals are identical, no two marriages will follow the exact same course. When heeded with an open heart, marriage advice can serve as a lighthouse, providing illumination and guidance without dictating the course.

In conclusion, marriage advice and well-wishes are integral to the marital journey. They are the treasures passed down through time, the compass guiding couples through uncharted waters, and the echoes of love and support resonating from the shores of family and friends. As couples embark on this shared odyssey, they are encouraged to weave these pieces of advice and well-wishes into the fabric of their union, creating a home rich in love, understanding, and shared joy.

Messages

V1. May Your Love Be Evergreen (#051)

As you embark on this journey of marriage, may your love be like an evergreen tree, steadfast and resilient through every season. Nurture it with patience, understanding, and shared laughter. Remember, just as the tree grows stronger with time, so too will your bond flourish with the experiences you weather together. May your love be a source of shade in times of heat and a shelter during life's storms.

V2. *Build a Home, Not Just a House* (#052)

Marriage is not just about sharing a living space; it's about creating a home filled with warmth, love, and understanding. As you build your life together, focus on nurturing a space where each of you feels accepted, cherished, and supported. Let your home be a sanctuary where you find solace in each other's arms and where the echoes of laughter create a symphony of shared joy.

V3. *Dance Through Life's Melody Together* (#053)

Marriage is a dance; life's music can sometimes have unexpected tempos. Embrace the rhythm of your shared journey, holding each other close through both the slow, romantic waltzes and the lively, energetic twists and turns. Remember, a successful dance requires communication, compromise, and a willingness to move in harmony. May your marriage be a beautiful and graceful dance that continues to evolve with every step.

V4. *Weather the Storms and Chase Rainbows* (#054)

Life is unpredictable, and storms may arise, but true love stands resilient in the face of challenges. As you navigate the ups and downs, remember that storms eventually pass, making way for rainbows. Cherish the moments of sunshine and appreciate the beauty that follows the rain. May your marriage be a testament to the strength that comes from facing challenges together and the beauty that emerges after the storm.

V5. *Sow Seeds of Friendship* (#055)

In the garden of marriage, friendship is the soil from which love blossoms. Cultivate a deep and enduring friendship with your spouse, nurturing it with trust, respect, and shared interests. Just as a garden requires attention and care, so does marriage. Water it with open communication, fertilize it with laughter, and watch as the seeds of your friendship grow into a beautiful, flourishing partnership. May your marriage be a garden that continually blooms with love, understanding, and companionship.

Quotes on Love and Marriage

- "Where there is love, there is life." – Mahatma Gandhi

- "You know you're in love when you can't fall asleep because reality is finally better than your dreams." – Dr. Seuss.

- "Unless you love someone, nothing else makes sense." – E.E. Cummings.

- "Love recognizes no barriers. It jumps hurdles, leaps fences, penetrates walls to arrive at its destination full of hope." – Maya Angelou.

- "Being deeply loved by someone gives you strength while loving someone deeply gives you courage." – Lao Tzu.

- "What greater thing is there for two human souls than to feel that they are joined for life–to strengthen each other in all labor, to rest on each other in all sorrow, to minister to each other in silent, unspeakable memories at the moment of the last parting?" – George Eliot

- "To love and be loved is to feel the sun from both sides." – David Viscott.

- "When you realize you want to spend the rest of your life with somebody, you want the rest of your life to start as soon as possible." – "When Harry Met Sally"

- "Love doesn't just sit there, like a stone, it has to be made, like bread; remade all the time, made new." – Ursula K. Le Guin, The Lathe of Heaven.

- "When I saw you, I fell in love, and you smiled because you knew." – Arrigo Boito.

- "A great marriage is not when the 'perfect couple' comes together. It is when an imperfect couple learns to enjoy their differences." – Dave Meurer.

- "There is no more lovely, friendly, and charming relationship, communion or company than a good marriage." – Martin Luther.

- "There is no remedy for love but to love more." – Henry David Thoreau.

- "Love at first sight is easy to understand; it's when two people have been looking at each other for a lifetime that it becomes a miracle." – Sam Levenson.

- "A happy marriage is a long conversation which always seems too short." – Andre Marois.

- "One word frees us of all the weight and pain of life: That word is love." – Sophocles

- "This is what we call love. When you are loved, you can do anything in creation. When you are loved, there's no need at all to understand what's happening because everything happens within you." – Paulo Coelho, The Alchemist.

- "For it was not into my ear you whispered, but into my heart. It was not my lips you kissed, but my soul." – Judy Garland.

- "When you trip over love, it is easy to get up. But when you fall in love, it is impossible to stand again." – Albert Einstein.

- "When we are in love, we open to all that life has to offer with passion, excitement, and acceptance." – John Lennon.

- "Doubt thou the stars are fire; Doubt that the sun doth move; Doubt truth to be a liar; But never doubt I love." – William Shakespeare.

- "The real act of marriage takes place in the heart, not in the ballroom or church or synagogue. It's a choice you make – not just on your wedding day, but over and over again – and that choice is reflected in the way you treat your husband or wife." – Barbara de Angelis.

- "In your light, I learn how to love. In your beauty, how to make poems. You dance inside my chest where no one sees you, but sometimes I do, and that sight becomes this art." – Rumi.

- "For you see, each day I love you more Today, more than yesterday and less than tomorrow." – Rosemonde Gerard.

- "To be fully seen by somebody, then, and be loved anyhow–this is a human offering that can border on miraculous." – Elizabeth Gilbert, Committed: A Skeptic Makes Peace with Marriage.

- "Love is life. And if you miss love, you miss life." – Leo Buscaglia.

- "I love you, not only for what you are but for what I am when I am with you. I love you, not only for what you have made of yourself but for what you are making of me."– Roy Croft.

- "To find someone who will love you for no reason, and to shower that person with reasons, that is the ultimate happiness." – Robert Brault.

- "In all the world, there is no heart for me like yours. In all the world, there is no love for you like mine." – Maya Angelou.

- "Love doesn't make the world go round. Love is what makes the ride worthwhile."– Franklin P. Jones

- "In the arithmetic of love, one plus one equals everything, and two minus one equals nothing."– Mignon McLaughlin.

- "Walking with your hands in mine and mine in yours, that's exactly where I want to be always."– Fawn Weaver

- "In dreams and in love, there are no impossibilities."– Janos Arnay.

- "The highest happiness on earth is the happiness of marriage." – William Lyon Phelps.

- "If I were to live a thousand years, I would belong to you for all of them. If we were to live a thousand lives, I would want to make you mine in each one." – Michelle Hodkin, The Evolution of Mara Dyer.

- "We loved with a love that was more than love." – Edgar Allan Poe, "Annabel Lee"

- "Is love this misguided need to have you beside me most of the time? Is love this safety I feel in our silences? Is it this belonging, this completeness?" – Chimamanda Ngozi Adichie, Half of a Yellow Sun

- "The best thing to hold onto in life is each other." – Audrey Hepburn.

- "He looked at her the way all women want to be looked at by a man." – F. Scott Fitzgerald.

- "So, I love you because the entire universe conspired to help me find you." — Paulo Coehlo

- "You don't love someone for their looks, or their clothes or for their fancy car, but because they sing a song only you can hear." — Oscar Wilde.

- "It was love at first sight, at last sight, at ever and ever sight." — Vladimir Nabokov, Lolita.

- "Two hearts can enlighten the whole world." — Sir Kristian Goldmund Aumann

- "Two hearts in love need no words." —Marceline Desbordes-Valmore.

- "Life is the flower for which love is the honey." — Victor Hugo.

- "True love stories never have endings." — Richard Bach.

- "To live without loving is to not really live." — Molière.

- "Insomuch as love grows in you, so beauty grows. For love is the beauty of the soul." — St. Augustine.

- "That love is all there is; that is all we know of love." — Emily Dickinson.

- "There is only one happiness in life: to love and be loved." — George Sand.

NEW HOME

A big change happens in your life when you move into a new home. You might feel a mix of excitement, hope, and a little longing for the familiar. At that point, the walls are more than just stone and brick. They are like empty vessels ready to be filled with memories, laughter, and the sounds of a well-lived life. Sending someone well wishes in their new home is a chance to say more than just nice things; it's a chance to get to the heart of this life-changing event.

To really wish someone well in their new home, you need to mix warmth, truthfulness, and a bit of hope. Start by recognizing the move's real and imagined parts: the new place they can shape and the emotional journey that comes with starting over. A heartfelt message knows how important this moment is and celebrates the building and the hopes, dreams, and fresh starts that the home stands for.

Comfort and safety might be good things to include in your wishes. Say that you hope every part of their new home will become a safe place where they can find comfort, joy, and a break from the stresses of the outside world. Stress that a home is more than just a place; it reflects who you are and a blank canvas ready to be filled with your style and attitude.

In addition, it gives off an air of growth and wealth. A new home is more than just a change of address; it symbolizes the fertile ground where dreams take root and blossom. Wish for the rooms to be filled with laughter, the halls with shared moments, and the doors open to a future marked by success and fulfillment. A touch of optimism can infuse the recipient with the confidence to embrace the chances and challenges of this fresh chapter.

When crafting your message, draw on shared memories and experiences if appropriate. Remind them that while the physical surroundings may be different, the emotional bonds and connections formed in the old space remain, transcending the limits of walls and distances. This acknowledgment of continuity can be a comforting memory amidst the novelty of a new environment.

Hence, wishing someone in their new home is not just about expressing good intentions; it's an art form that involves weaving emotions into words, creating a tapestry of hope, warmth, and encouragement. It's a gesture that extends beyond the housewarming gift, making the recipient feel seen, valued, and ready to start on this exciting trip. So, let your wishes resonate like the gentle hum of a house settling into its foundations, welcoming the promise of a beautiful, new beginning.

Housewarming Messages

Embarking on a new chapter in life, moving into a new home is a momentous occasion that beckons celebration and warm wishes. As friends, family, and loved ones step through the threshold of a freshly acquired space, the exchange of housewarming messages becomes a timeless tradition. Let's delve into the significance of housewarming messages, exploring the art of crafting sentiments that resonate with the joy, hope, and camaraderie inherent in such a transitional period.

Body:

Symbolism of Home: A home is more than just walls and a roof; it is a sanctuary, a canvas for memories, and a reflection of one's identity. Housewarming messages serve as acknowledgments of this profound symbolism, offering heartfelt congratulations on creating a new haven.

Conveying Warmth and Well-Wishes: Housewarming messages are more than just customary pleasantries – they are expressions of warmth and genuine goodwill. In these messages, friends and family convey their hopes for comfort, happiness, and prosperity in the new abode, creating positive energy for the homeowners.

Personalization and Thoughtfulness: Crafting an effective housewarming message involves a touch of personalization and thoughtfulness. Recognizing the unique taste and style of the new home, a well-crafted message reflects the sender's understanding and appreciation for the homeowners' journey.

Offering Practical and Emotional Support: Beyond the celebratory aspect, housewarming messages can extend practical and emotional support. Sharing tips on settling in, offering assistance with the transition, or simply expressing a willingness to lend a helping hand creates a sense of community and shared responsibility.

Honoring Tradition and Culture: Housewarming messages often incorporate elements of tradition and culture. Whether it's a heartfelt blessing, a symbol of good luck, or a cultural reference, these messages become a bridge that connects the old with the new, preserving and passing on cherished customs.

Strengthening Bonds: Housewarming messages serve as a thread that weaves through the tapestry of relationships. By crafting a meaningful message, the sender strengthens the bonds of friendship and family, reinforcing the idea that a home is not just a physical space but a gathering place for loved ones.

Woven with care and sincerity, housewarming messages enrich this narrative by adding layers of joy, positivity, and connection. As we extend our wishes and congratulations, we celebrate the physical space and the emotions, dreams, and aspirations that make a house a home.

Messages

V1. Warmest Wishes for Your New Nest (#056)

Congratulations on your beautiful new home! May every room be filled with love, laughter, and cherished moments. Here's to creating a haven of joy and making countless memories in your new abode. Best wishes for a cozy and wonderful chapter ahead.

V2. A Home Full of Happiness (#057)

As you step into this new chapter of your life, may your home be a sanctuary of happiness and love. May the walls echo with laughter, and each corner be a witness to the warmth of family and friends. Wishing you endless joy, comfort, and unforgettable moments in your new home.

V3. Building Dreams and Creating Memories (#058)

Congratulations on the keys to your new kingdom! May your home be a canvas for painting beautiful memories and a fortress for nurturing dreams. Here's to the countless gatherings, shared meals, and the love that will fill every nook and cranny. May this new adventure be everything you've ever wished for and more.

V4. *Opening the Door to a New Chapter* (#059)

Stepping into a new home is like opening the door to a new chapter in the story of your life. May each day in your new abode be a page filled with joy, love, and exciting adventures. Wishing you the happiest of housewarmings and a future filled with warmth and cherished moments.

V5. *Home is Where the Heart Is* (#060)

Congratulations on finding your perfect haven! May your new home be a reflection of your dreams and a place where your heart feels truly content. Here's to the countless sunsets from your porch, shared meals in your kitchen, and the love that will fill every room. May your home be a sanctuary of peace and joy for years to come.

Quotes for a New Home

- "The ache for home lives in all of us. The safe place where we can go as we are and not be questioned." — **Maya Angelou**

- "We shape our dwellings, and afterward, our dwellings shape us." — **Winston Churchill.**

- "There is nothing like staying at home for real comfort." — **Jane Austen.**

- "A table, a chair, a bowl of fruit, and a violin; what else does a man need to be happy?" — **Albert Einstein.**

- "The best and most beautiful things in the world cannot be seen or even touched – they must be felt with the heart." — **Helen Keller.**

- "A house is not just a place to live; it is a work of art in which we create our own stories." — **Frank Lloyd Wright.**

- "Home is where you feel at ease and comfortable, where you can be yourself without judgment." — **Ernest Hemingway.**

- "Home is where your story begins." — **J.K. Rowling.**

- "A house is not a home unless it contains food and fire for the mind as well as the body." — **Benjamin Franklin.**

- "Every house has its own soul, its own character. Make sure that your house has a soul which is in harmony with your own soul!" — **Mehmet Murat Ildan.**

- "The time to repair the roof is when the sun is shining." — **John F. Kennedy.**

- "I put all my genius into my life; I put only my talent into my works." — **Oscar Wilde.**

- "As we let our light shine, we unconsciously permit other people to do the same. As we are liberated from our own fear, our presence automatically liberates others." — **Marianne Williamson.**

May your new home be filled with joy, laughter, and the warmth of cherished moments.

GRADUATION

As the tassels are turned, the caps are thrown into the air, and the echoes of "Pomp and Circumstance" fade away, the significance of graduation becomes abundantly clear. It is a moment that encapsulates the culmination of years of hard work, dedication, and growth. The air is thick with a mixture of excitement, nostalgia, and perhaps a touch of apprehension as graduates stand at the threshold of a new chapter in their lives. In these moments, graduation wishes take on a profound role—they are not merely expressions of congratulation but reflections of support, encouragement, and hope for the journey that lies ahead.

Graduation wishes are not just casual phrases exchanged in passing; they are thoughtful messages that carry the weight of acknowledgment for the challenges overcome, the knowledge gained, and the personal transformations experienced. These wishes serve as beacons of recognition, signaling to the graduates that their efforts have not gone unnoticed and their achievements have left an indelible mark on those who have witnessed their journey.

One of the primary aspects of graduation wishes is the celebration of accomplishments. Whether it be the completion of high school, college, or a specialized program, each graduation is a testament to the individual's resilience, determination, and tenacity. Wishes at this juncture often weave words of praise, recognizing the academic achievements, leadership roles, and extracurricular triumphs that have shaped the graduates into the person they have become. It is an acknowledgment of the countless hours spent in libraries, laboratories, or studios – a recognition of the dedication to the pursuit of knowledge and personal growth.

However, beyond celebrating academic success, graduation wishes to carry a deeper layer of sentiment. They extend beyond the confines of transcripts and diplomas, delving into character, integrity, and the qualities that make an individual truly remarkable. These wishes become an avenue to express admiration for the kindness shown, the friendships forged, and the positive impact the graduate has had on those around them. They are an affirmation that success is not measured solely by grades but also by the meaningful connections formed and the positive influence left in the wake of one's educational journey.

In essence, graduation wishes to bridge the past and the future. They encapsulate the sentiment that a new adventure is on the horizon while the academic chapter may be closing. Whether it is stepping into the workforce, pursuing further education, or embarking on a unique path, graduates are met with a mixture of possibilities and uncertainties. Wishes at this juncture become words of encouragement, offering a gentle push towards the uncharted territories that await. They convey the belief that the skills acquired, the lessons learned, and the resilience developed during the academic journey will serve as invaluable companions in navigating the world's complexities beyond the classroom.

Moreover, graduation wishes often carry an undertone of optimism. They remind us that, despite the challenges that may lie ahead, the graduates possess the strength, knowledge, and adaptability to overcome whatever obstacles come their way. These wishes are not just formalities but expressions of faith in the potential and capacity of the graduates to make meaningful contributions to society, effect positive change, and carve out a path uniquely their own.

Hence, graduation wishes are more than just congratulatory expressions; they are nuanced, heartfelt messages that encapsulate the essence of the educational journey. They are a celebration of achievements, a recognition of character, and a guiding light for the journey ahead.

Graduation Congratulations

Graduation is an important life milestone, and everyone should say, "Congratulations, Graduate!" But what should you put in a graduation letter to best communicate how extremely happy you are about this years-long accomplishment, whether from high school or college? We're here to help with samples of personal notes, ranging from sweet to hilarious, that you may choose from or customize to build your own. Whichever one you choose, it will add the perfect inspirational touch to a financial gift in the form of a card or a special present chosen to remember your graduate's accomplishments and their new chapter.

Messages

V1. Celebrating Your Achievement: A Hearty Congratulations on Your Graduation! (#061)

As you stand at the threshold of this significant accomplishment, we extend our warmest congratulations to you on your graduation day. Your dedication, perseverance, and hard work have paid off, and today marks the culmination of a remarkable journey. May this be just the beginning of an exciting chapter filled with continued success, personal growth, and the pursuit of your dreams. Your achievements are an inspiration to us all, and we look forward to witnessing the incredible impact you will undoubtedly make on the world.

V2. *Commencing a New Chapter: Heartfelt Congratulations on Your Graduation!* (#062)

With immense joy and pride, we extend our heartfelt congratulations on your graduation. This momentous achievement is a testament to your unwavering commitment to excellence and the pursuit of knowledge. As you step into the next phase of your life, may the skills and wisdom you've gained during your academic journey guide you toward a future filled with limitless possibilities. Embrace the challenges, savor the victories, and continue to strive for greatness. Your graduation is not just an end but the commencement of a new and exciting chapter in your remarkable story.

V3. *The World Awaits: Congratulations on Your Well-Earned Graduation!* (#063)

Congratulations on reaching this incredible milestone! Your graduation is a reflection of your academic prowess and a celebration of your resilience, determination, and the countless hard work you've dedicated to your studies. As you embark on the journey beyond academia, remember that the world awaits your unique talents and contributions. May this graduation be the launching pad for a future brimming with success, fulfillment, and the realization of your most ambitious aspirations. Well done, and here's to the promising adventures that lie ahead!

V4. *Diploma in Hand, Dreams in Heart: Warm Congratulations on Graduating!* (#064)

Today, we celebrate not just the receipt of a diploma but the culmination of your tireless efforts and intellectual growth. Your graduation is a testament to your ability to overcome challenges, persevere in the face of adversity, and emerge victorious. As you stand on the cusp of a promising future, take pride in your accomplishments and carry the lessons learned into the next chapter of your life. Heartfelt congratulations on your graduation, and may the journey ahead be as extraordinary as the one that brought you to this significant milestone.

V5. *A Resounding Bravo: Congratulations on Your Graduation Achievement!* (#065)

Bravo! Your graduation is a resounding achievement that resonates with your dedication and commitment to your education. As you stand on the stage of accomplishment, know that this is just the prologue to a narrative of continued success and personal fulfillment. The applause is not only for the cap and gown but for the knowledge gained, the obstacles conquered, and the growth experienced. Congratulations on this momentous occasion, and may your post-graduation journey be as bright and inspiring as your academic endeavors have been.

Inspirational Quotes for Graduates

Finding the proper graduation quote can be a time-consuming task. After four years of hard effort, you want to mark this significant occasion with the appropriate words. Something that defines your identity and establishes the tone for the future. Graduating requires a lot of blood, sweat, tears, and ramen—especially after nearly two years of distance learning.

But the time has come for you to wear your hard-earned graduation robes, decorate your cap, and rewatch your favorite graduation movies to prepare for the big day. Wear your tassel proudly, and, of course, select the appropriate phrase for graduation Instagrams. You didn't study so hard in school simply to publish a captionless photo, right?

From Taylor Swift's motivating comments to Ariana Grande's wise remarks, below is a compilation of a list of the best graduation quotes from celebrities, athletes, politicians, writers, cartoon characters, and more. These meaningful pieces of advice are ideal for use in graduation cards, commencement speeches, or as inspirational senior quotes in your yearbook. The choice is yours!

High School Graduation Quotes

- "Your life is your adventure. And the adventure ahead of you is a journey to fulfill your own purpose and potential." —Kerry Washington.

- "If you can do what you do best and be happy, you are further along in life than most people." —Leonardo DiCaprio.

- "Education is the most powerful weapon we can use to change the world." —Nelson Mandela.

- "Your education is a dress rehearsal for a life that is yours to lead." —Nora Ephron.

- "You are about to start the greatest improvisation of all. With no script. No idea what's going to happen, often with people and places you have never seen before. And you are not in control. So say 'yes.' And if you're lucky, you'll find people who will say 'yes' back." —Stephen Colbert

- "You must have some vision for your life. Even if you don't know the plan, you have to have a direction in which you choose to go." —Oprah.

- "You don't go to university, so you can punch a clock. You go to university so you can be in a position to make a difference." —Janet Napolitano.

- "Education is our passport to the future, for tomorrow belongs to the people who prepare for it today." —Malcolm X.

- "I've learned it's important not to limit yourself. You can do whatever you really love to do, no matter what it is." —Ryan Gosling.

- "Fight for what makes you optimistic about the world. Find it, insist on it, dig into it, go after it." —Jennifer Garner.

- "Intelligence plus character—that is the goal of true education." —Martin Luther King Jr.

- "You cannot dream of becoming something you do not know about. You have to learn to dream big. Education exposes you to what the world has to offer, to the possibilities open to you." —Sonia Sotomayor.

- "If I must give any of you advice, it would be to say yes. Say yes, and create your own destiny." —Maya Rudolph.

- "Your inexperience is an asset in that it will make you think in original, unconventional ways. Accept your lack of knowledge and use it as your asset." —Natalie Portman.

- "Take your risks now. As you grow older, you become more fearful and less flexible … Try to keep your mind open to possibilities and your mouth closed on matters that you don't know about. Limit your 'always' and your 'nevers.' Continue to share your heart with people even if it's been broken." —Amy Poehler

- "You can't connect the dots looking forward; you can only connect them looking backward. You have to trust that the dots will somehow connect in your future." —Steve Jobs.

- "Now go, and make interesting mistakes, make amazing mistakes, make glorious and fantastic mistakes. Break rules. Leave the world more interesting for your being here." —Neil Gaiman.

- "When you respect the idea that you are sharing the Earth with other humans, and when you lead with your nice foot forward, you'll win, every time. It might not be today, it might not be tomorrow, but it comes back to you when you need it." —Kristen Bell.

- "Be thankful for what you have; you'll end up having more. If you concentrate on what you don't have you, you will never, ever have enough." —Oprah.

- "He who is not courageous enough to take risks will accomplish nothing in life." —Muhammad Ali.

- "Go make your big beautiful dent, and as you do so come down on the side of boldness. If you err, may it be for too much audacity and not too little. For you really are enough. You have untold strengths and resources inside. You have your glorious self." —Sue Monk Kidd.

- "It is often easier to make progress on mega-ambitious dreams. I know that sounds completely nuts. But, since no one else is crazy enough to do it, you have little competition." —Larry Page.

- "Some life lessons don't ever change. They need to be highlighted and they need to be remembered throughout our entire lives. But how you embrace them will distinguish you from the pack." —Brooke Shields.

- "You and you alone are the only person who can live the life that writes the story that you were meant to tell." — Kerry Washington.

- "Be the hardest working person you know. Because if you're not, someone else will be." —Ian Brennan

- "In response to those who say to stop dreaming and face reality, I say keep dreaming and make reality." —Kristian Kan.

- "It's your turn to choose and define what success means to you. Now, others will try to define it for you, but yours is the only voice that matters." — Octavia Spencer.

- Nobody else is paying as much attention to your failures as you are . . . to everyone else, it's just a blip on the radar screen, so just move on. —Jerry Zucker

- "I am here to tell you that whatever you think your dream is now, it will probably change. And that's okay." —Conan O'Brien.

- "Learn from every mistake because every experience, encounter, and particularly your mistakes are there to teach you and force you into being more who you are. And then figure out what is the next right move. And the key to life is to develop an internal moral, emotional G.P.S. that can tell you which way to go." —Oprah.

- "If we'd all stuck with our first dream, the world would be overrun with cowboys and princesses. So whatever your dream is right now if you don't achieve it, you haven't failed, and you're not some loser." —Stephen Colbert.

- "Don't be afraid of fear. Because it sharpens you, it challenges you, it makes you stronger; and when you run away from fear, you also run away from the opportunity to be your best possible self."—Ed Helms.

Funny Graduation Quotes

- "We're only here for so long. Be happy, man. You could get hit by a truck tomorrow." —Timothée Chalamet.

- "Don't allow people to dim your shine because they are blinded. Tell them to put on sunglasses." —Lady Gaga.

- "Get busy living or get busy dying." —Stephen King

- "You can't climb the ladder of success with your hands in your pockets." —Arnold Schwarzenegger.

- "If you aren't going all the way, why go at all?" —Joe Namath

- "You miss 100% of the shots you don't take." —Wayne Gretzky.

- "You will stumble and fall, you will experience both disaster and triumph, sometimes in the same day. But it's really important to remember that like a hangover, neither triumphs nor disasters last forever." —Helen Mirren.

- "Opportunity is missed by most people because it is dressed in overalls and looks like work." —Thomas Edison.

- "You have to dance a little bit before you step out into the world each day, because it changes the way you walk." —Sandra Bullock.

- "Even if you are on the right track, you will get run over if you just sit there." —Will Rogers.

- "The road to success is always under construction." —Lily Tomlin.

- "You're only given a little spark of madness. You mustn't lose it." —Robin Williams.

- "Opportunity dances with those who are already on the dance floor." —Jackson Browne

College Graduation Quotes

- "Success is nothing if you don't have the right people to share it with; you're just going to end up lonely." —Selena Gomez.

- "The meaning of life is to find your gift, the purpose of life is to give it away." —Joy J. Golliver.

- "That clock you hear is the sound of your own heart. Sink your teeth into this life, and don't get let go." —Lin-Manuel Miranda.

- "No job or task is too small or beneath you. If you want to get ahead, volunteer to do the things no one else wants to do, and do it better." —Bobbi Brown

- "You can't do it alone. Be open to collaboration. Find a group of people who challenge and inspire you. Spend a lot of time with them and it will change your life." — Amy Poehler.

- "When we show up, act boldly, and practice the best ways to be wrong, we fail forward. No matter where we end up, we've grown from where we began." —Stacey Abrams.

- "I celebrate you as you remember the power of grace and pride, and I challenge you to choose freedom over fear." —Janelle Monáe.

- "Education is not preparation for life; education is life itself." —John Dewey.

- "You could travel with the sheep, follow everybody else's stuff, but then you're not you. I guess if I want to say anything, it's 'Be you.' Be true to you, and that should make the ride a little more interesting." — Whoopi Goldberg

- "There will be times when your best isn't good enough. There can be many reasons for this, but as long as you give your best, you'll be okay." —Robert De Niro.

- "We may live in an age of instant messaging, instant gratification and Instagram, but there is no way to short circuit the path to success." —Tory Burch.

- "Now the first suggestion is to aim high, but be aware that even before you have reached your ultimate professional destination, if you always strive for excellence, you can and should have a substantial impact on the world in which you live." —Sandra Day O'Connor.

- "As you graduate, as you deal with your excitement and your doubts today, I urge you to try and create the world you want to live in. Minister to the world in a way that can change it. Minister radically in a real, active, practical, get your hands dirty way." —Chimamanda Ngozi Adichie.

- "Go confidently in the direction of your dreams. Live the life you have imagined." —Henry David Thoreau.

- "The horizon leans forward, offering you space to place new steps of change." —Maya Angelou.

- "There is nothing more beautiful than finding your course as you believe you bob aimlessly in the current. Wouldn't you know that your path was there all along, waiting for you to knock, waiting for you to become. This path does not belong to your parents, your teachers, your leaders, or your lovers. Your path is your character defining itself more and more everyday like a photograph coming into focus." —Jodie Foster.

- "Real leadership comes from the quiet nudging of an inner voice. It comes from realizing that the time has come to move beyond waiting to doing." —Madeleine Albright.

- "Dreams are lovely. But they are just dreams. Fleeting, ephemeral, pretty. But dreams do not come true just because you dream them. It's hard work that makes things happen. It's hard work that creates change." —Shonda Rhimes.

- "Don't just get involved. Fight for your seat at the table. Better yet, fight for a seat at the head of the table." —Barack Obama.

Inspirational Graduation Quotes

- "We are all deserving, and we don't need permission or an invitation to exist and to step into our power." —Ilhan Omar

- "Your self worth is determined by you. You don't have to depend on someone telling you who you are." —Beyoncé.

- "No matter what happens in life, be good to people. Being good to people is a wonderful legacy to leave behind." —Taylor Swift.

- "There's something so special about a woman who dominates in a man's world. It takes a certain grace, strength, intelligence, fearlessness, and the nerve to never take no for an answer." —Rihanna.

- "Understand that one day you will have the power to make a difference, so use it well." —Mindy Kaling

- "I'm continually trying to make choices that put me out of my own comfort zone. As long as you're uncomfortable, it means you're growing." —Ashton Kutcher

- "It's amazing what you can get if you quietly, clearly and authoritatively demand it." —Meryl Streep.

- "It's the choice. You have to wake up every day and say, 'There's no reason today can't be the best day of my life.'" —Blake Lively

- "I've failed over and over and over again in my life. And that is why I succeed." —Michael Jordan.

- "There may be people that have more talent than you, but there's no excuse for anyone to work harder than you do." —Derek Jeter.

- "My favorite animal is the turtle. The reason is that in order for the turtle to move, it has to stick its neck out. There are going to be times in your life when you're going to have to stick your neck out. There will be challenges, and instead of hiding in a shell, you have to go out and meet them." —Ruth Westheimer.

- "There is no passion to be found in playing small — in settling for a life that is less than the one you are capable of living." —Nelson Mandela.

- "When someone who loves you hugs you, hug them back with two arms—don't do the one-arm hug, because when you hug someone with two arms, it allows you to lean on somebody, and we all need someone to lean on." — Sandra Bullock.

- "Frustration, although quite painful at times, is a very positive and essential part of success. —Bo Bennett

- "You can never be the best. The only thing you can be the best at is developing yourself." — Natalie Portman.

- "Real courage is holding on to a still voice in your head that says, 'I must keep going.' It's that voice that says nothing is a failure if it is not final. That voice that says to you, 'Get out of bed. Keep going. I will not quit.'" —Cory Booker

- "Cynicism has never won a war, or cured a disease, or started a business, or fed a young mind, or sent men into space. Cynicism is a choice. Hope is a better choice." —Barack Obama.

- "What lies behind us and what lies before us are small matters compared to what lies within us." —Ralph Waldo Emerson

- "When people tell you not to believe in your dreams, and they say 'Why?' say 'Why not?'" —Billie Jean King

- "I encourage you to live with life. Be courageous and adventurous. Give us a tomorrow, more than we deserve." —Maya Angelou

- "There is no such thing as failure. Failure is just life trying to move us in another direction." — Oprah Winfrey.

- "I'm a greater believer in luck, and I find the harder I work, the more I have of it." —Thomas Jefferson.

Short Graduation Quotes

- "Change takes courage." —Alexandria Ocasio-Cortez

- "You're never a loser until you quit trying." —Mike Ditka

- "Your imagination is your preview of life's coming attractions." —Albert Einstein

- "Work so hard that you never have to introduce yourself." —Gigi Hadid

- "It's hard to beat a person who never gives up." —Babe Ruth

- "There are no regrets in life — just lessons." —Jennifer Aniston

- "Stay hungry. Stay foolish." —Steven Jobs

- "A woman with a voice is, by definition, a strong woman." —Melinda Gates

- "You get in life what you have the courage to ask for." —Oprah Winfrey

- "To give any less than your best is to sacrifice a gift." —Steve Prefontaine

- "Being realistic is the most commonly traveled road to mediocrity." —Will Smith

- "Persistence can change failure into extraordinary achievement." —Matt Bondi

- "If you can't outplay them, outwork them." —Ben Hogan

- "This above all: To thine own self be true." —William Shakespeare

- "Do. Or do not. There is no try." —Yoda

- "Be bold, be courageous, be your best." –Gabrielle Giffords

- "It is absolutely still possible to make a difference." —Michelle Obama

Wisdom for the Next Chapter

Graduation marks the end of one chapter and the beginning of another. As we stand on the precipice of the unknown, the journey ahead may seem both exhilarating and daunting. This transition from the familiar halls of academia to the uncharted territories of adulthood calls for a dose of wisdom to navigate the twists and turns that await.

Firstly, embrace the beauty of learning beyond the classroom. Graduation isn't the end of education; it's a shift from textbooks to life lessons. Each experience, whether big or small, offers an opportunity to gain insights and hone your understanding of the world. Approach every challenge with an open mind, ready to absorb the wisdom that comes with navigating the complexities of the real world.

In this next chapter, remember the importance of resilience. Life has a tendency to present unexpected challenges and setbacks, but it is our ability to bounce back that defines our journey. Learn from failures, celebrate small victories, and keep moving forward. As J.K. Rowling once said, "It is impossible to live without failing at something unless you live so cautiously that you might as well not have lived at all."

Developing a strong sense of self-awareness is another cornerstone of wisdom. Take the time to understand your strengths, weaknesses, and passions. Recognize that it's okay not to have all the answers right away. The journey of self-discovery is ongoing, and as you encounter different facets of life, you'll uncover more layers of your own identity.

Moreover, cherish relationships and nurture meaningful connections. Your journey is not solitary, and the people you meet along the way contribute immensely to your growth. Surround yourself with individuals who inspire, challenge, and support you. Build a network of diverse relationships that enrich your life with a variety of perspectives.

Financial literacy is a practical aspect of wisdom that often gets overlooked. Understand the value of budgeting, saving, and investing early on. No matter how small, financial decisions have a cumulative impact on your future. Equip yourself with the knowledge to make informed choices that contribute to your long-term well-being.

Lastly, never underestimate the power of kindness. In a world that can sometimes be harsh, a compassionate and empathetic heart will benefit others and bring fulfillment to your own life. No matter how small, acts of kindness create ripples that extend far beyond the immediate moment.

As you embark on the next chapter after graduation, remember that wisdom is not a destination but a continuous journey. Embrace the unknown with curiosity, resilience, and an open heart. Life's lessons are abundant, and with each passing day, you have the opportunity to accumulate a wealth of wisdom that shapes your unique story.

RETIREMENT

Retirement marks a significant chapter in a person's life, signaling the conclusion of a dedicated career and the commencement of a new, uncharted journey. It is a moment of profound transition, ripe with emotions ranging from nostalgia to excitement, as one reflects on the past and anticipates the limitless possibilities of the future. Wishing someone a happy retirement is not merely a formality; it is an expression of appreciation, admiration, and heartfelt encouragement for the adventures that lie ahead.

At its core, a retirement wish is a celebration of a life well-lived. It encapsulates the years of hard work, dedication, and resilience that have shaped the retiree's professional identity and personal growth. In offering retirement wishes, we acknowledge the individual's unique contributions, their impact on colleagues and the organization, and their lasting legacy.

One commonly wishes for a retirement filled with relaxation and leisure, and rightly so. After years of adhering to schedules, deadlines, and professional responsibilities, retirees deserve the luxury of time to pursue hobbies, spend with loved ones, and explore passions that may have been put on hold. Retirement wishes often carry the hope for abundant joy, tranquility, and the freedom to savor life's simple pleasures.

However, retirement is not just about bidding farewell to the workplace but about embracing new beginnings. A well-crafted retirement wish recognizes the potential for continued growth, learning, and discovery in this next phase of life. It encourages the retiree to see retirement not as an end but as a fresh start, an opportunity to redefine oneself and explore uncharted territories.

Moreover, a retirement wish serves as a bridge between the past and the future. It offers gratitude for the journey so far, acknowledging the challenges overcome and the milestones achieved. At the same time, it extends support and optimism for the adventures awaiting the retiree in the years to come. The sentiment says, "Thank you for your dedicated service, and may the best of life's offerings accompany you in your retirement."

In essence, wishing someone a happy retirement is an artful blend of reflection, appreciation, and anticipation. It is an acknowledgment of the retiree's past achievements, an expression of good wishes for their well-deserved relaxation, and an encouragement for the exciting possibilities that lie ahead. As we extend our heartfelt retirement wishes, we witness the seamless transition from one fulfilling chapter to the promising pages of the next.

Congratulations on Retirement

Retirement is a significant event in our lives and should be acknowledged in the workplace. However, while planning to connect over this milestone, remember that people retire for various reasons, so there is no one-size-fits-all message.

When deciding how to recognize the retirement of a friend, coworker, or client, consider why they are retiring. When contemplating the "why," writing a genuine and heartfelt retirement card message becomes much easier.

Retirement is a choice. Your colleague, coworker, friend, or client has worked for many years and can afford to retire, or they have accepted an early

68

retirement package as part of a firm downsizing. Consider the emotional intricacies of both instances, but in both cases, the person will most likely be moving on to other things they want to do. They typically look forward to hobbies, volunteer activities, vacations, family time, and other professional interests.

Retirement owing to other reasons. Other causes for retirement include legislated retirement age ceilings or union retirement eligibility after 20 years on the job. In the latter situation, you can have someone who is relatively young changing careers or finding a new method to apply their expertise. Finally, it is not rare for people to retire to address their own or other family members' health difficulties. Regardless of the circumstances, retirement is a significant milestone to mark.

Messages

V1. For a Long-Serving Employee (#066)

Congratulations on reaching this incredible milestone of retirement! Your dedication and hard work over the years have been an inspiration to us all. May your days ahead be filled with relaxation, joy, and the fulfillment of all your dreams. You've earned every moment of this new chapter. Happy retirement!

V2. For a Colleague and Friend (#067)

As you embark on this new adventure called retirement, I want you to know how much your friendship and camaraderie have meant to me at work. Wishing you endless days of laughter, exploration, and well-deserved relaxation. May this next chapter bring you all the happiness you've given to others. Cheers to your retirement!

V3. For the Team Player (#068)

To the one who always played a crucial role in our team's success – your retirement leaves a void that will be hard to fill. Thank you for your unwavering commitment and teamwork. May your retirement be as fulfilling and rewarding as your contributions to our projects. Enjoy every moment of this well-deserved break!

V4. For the Mentor (#069)

Retirement isn't the end; it's the beginning of a new journey. Your guidance and mentorship have shaped many careers, mine included. Wishing you a retirement filled with the same wisdom, warmth, and joy you've shared with us throughout your career. May this new chapter be your most fulfilling yet!

V5. For the Innovator (#070)

Your innovative spirit has been the driving force behind many of our successful projects. As you retire, may your creativity continue to blossom in new and exciting ways. Thank you for pushing boundaries and inspiring us all. Here's to a retirement filled with endless possibilities and continued brilliance!

V6. For the Team Leader (#071)

Leading with grace and expertise, you've been the anchor of our team. Your retirement leaves big shoes to fill, but your legacy will guide us forward. Wishing you a retirement filled with relaxation and the joy of knowing your leadership made a lasting impact. You will be missed, but your influence will endure.

V7. For the Hard Worker (#072)

Your strong work ethic and dedication have set a standard for all of us. As you retire, may you find time for the things you love and the relaxation you deserve. Your tireless efforts have not gone unnoticed, and your absence will be felt. Cheers to a retirement filled with well-earned rest and happiness!

V8. *For the Creative Mind* (#073)

Your creative spark has brought color and innovation to our workplace. As you step into retirement, may your days be filled with artistic inspiration and the freedom to explore new passions. Thank you for making our work environment richer with your imaginative contributions. Wishing you a retirement as vibrant as your creativity!

V9. *For the Problem Solver* (#074)

To the one who always found solutions even in the most challenging situations – your retirement is a well-deserved break from solving problems. May this next phase of life be free of challenges and full of the peace you've earned. Happy retirement to the one who always knew how to get things done!

V10. *For the Versatile Contributor* (#075)

Your ability to adapt and excel in various roles has been truly remarkable. As you retire, may your versatility continue to shine in whatever you choose to pursue. Your impact has been felt across departments, and your legacy will endure. I wish you a retirement as dynamic and fulfilling as your career!

User Quotes on the Joys of Retiring

- "To appreciate beauty; to find the best in others; to leave the world a bit better whether by a healthy child, a garden patch, or a redeemed social condition; to know that even one life has breathed easier because you have lived. This is to have succeeded." – Ralph Waldo Emerson.

- "It's not the days in life we remember, rather the moments." – Walt Disney.

- "And in the end, it's not the years in your life that count. It's the life in your years." – Abraham Lincoln

- "Life was meant to be lived, and curiosity must be kept alive. One must never, for whatever reason, turn his back on life." – Eleanor Roosevelt.

- "Life is not measured by the number of breaths we take, but by the moments that take our breath away." – Maya Angelou.

- "In all of living, have much fun and laughter. Life is to be enjoyed, not just endured." – Gordon B. Hinckley.

- "The first step to getting the things you want out of life is this: Decide what you want." – Ben Stein.

- "You are never too old to set a new goal or dream a new dream." – C.S. Lewis.

- "Do not grow old, no matter how long you live. Never cease to stand like curious children before the great mystery into which we were born." – Albert Einstein.

- "People will forget what you said, people will forget what you did, but people will never forget how you made them feel." – Maya Angelou.

- "There is a fountain of youth: it is your mind, your talents, the creativity you bring to your life and the lives of people you love. When you learn to tap this source, you will truly have defeated age." – Sophia Loren.

- "Have the courage to follow your heart and intuition. They somehow already know what you truly want…everything else is secondary." – Steve Jobs.

- "Don't think of retiring from the world until the world will be sorry that you retire." – Samuel Johnson.

- "The longer I live, the more beautiful life becomes." – Frank Lloyd Wright.

- "There are far better things ahead than we ever leave behind." – C.S. Lewis.

- "Retire from work, but not from life." – M.K. Soni.

- "The most important thing is to enjoy your life" – Audrey Hepburn.

- "Great is the art of beginning, but greater is the art of ending." – Henry Wadsworth Longfellow.

- "Often when you think you're at the end of something, you're at the beginning of something else." – Fred Rogers.

- "Every new beginning comes from some other beginning's end." – Dan Wilson.

- "Goodbyes make you think. They make you realize what you've had, what you've lost, and what you've taken for granted." – Ritu Ghatourey.

- "Age is an issue of mind over matter. If you don't mind, it doesn't matter." – Mark Twain.

- "There's one thing I always wanted to do before I quit . . . . retire!" – Groucho Marx.

- "There's never enough time to do all the nothing you want." – Bill Waterson.

- "Retirement: That's when you return from work one day and say, 'Hi honey, I'm home forever." – Gene Perret.

- "Working people have a lot of bad habits, but the worst of those is work." – Clarence Darrow.

- "Just living is not enough…..one must have sunshine, freedom, and a little flower." – Hans Christian Andersen.

- "Why are people afraid of getting older? You feel wiser. You feel more mature. You feel like you know yourself better. You would trade that for softer skin? Not me!" – Anna Kournikova.

- "We don't grow older, we grow riper." – Pablo Picasso.

- "Gainfully unemployed, very proud of it, too." – Charles Baxter.

- Retirement is wonderful. It's doing nothing without worrying about getting caught at it." – Gene Perret.

- "Getting old is like climbing a mountain; you get a little out of breath, but the view is much better!" – Ingrid Bergman.

SPECIAL HOLIDAYS

Celebrating special holidays is more than just exchanging gifts and decorating; it captures the essence of human connection and the warmth that comes with offering well-wishes. Whether it's Christmas, New Year's, birthdays, or other important occasions, sending customized holiday greetings is an art form that improves connections, encourages a sense of belonging, and generates lasting memories.

Acknowledging your shared joy is one of the most important components of wishing someone well on a special occasion. People gather to honor traditions, values, and meaningful memories during the holiday season. A thoughtful holiday wish serves as a bridge, bringing people together in a shared experience of celebration and joy. It means, "I recognize and honor the importance of this occasion in your life."

Furthermore, special holiday wishes communicate goodwill and pleasant energy. Whether offering heartfelt wishes for a Merry Christmas, a Happy New Year, or a pleasant birthday, these greetings express a sincere desire for happiness, prosperity, and fulfillment in the recipient's life. In a society frequently defined by hurry and bustle, expressing heartfelt wishes over the holidays builds a feeling of community. It reminds people of the inherent goodness in human interactions.

The act of wishing someone well on important occasions exemplifies the power of language to shape emotions. A well-crafted message can elicit excitement, thanks, and a sense of being valued. This linguistic creativity entails choosing words that reflect the individual's personality, the occasion's significance, and the relationship's depth. It elevates a simple wish to a meaningful declaration that resonates in the heart long after the Christmas season has ended.

Furthermore, special holiday greetings provide a time for introspection and mindfulness. Birthdays, for example, allow us to celebrate not only the passage of time but also the individual's growth, achievements, and resilience. New Year's wishes frequently express hopes, aspirations, and general optimism for the next year. In these moments, spreading well-wishes becomes a collaborative voyage of introspection and projection, reinforcing a sense of community and common goals.

To summarize, the art of wishing on special occasions goes beyond mere formality; it is a heartfelt statement of connection, goodwill, and shared joy. Individuals convey not only their current emotions but also their admiration for the connection and the distinctive features of the person they are celebrating, using carefully chosen words. Special holiday greetings are the threads that weave warmth, love, and shared experiences into the tapestry of human connection. They serve as a reminder that, amid life's craziness, taking the time to wish someone well is an act of generosity that resonates with the timeless echoes of human connection.

Examples of Special Holidays

Diwali

Diwali, known as the Festival of Lights, is a significant celebration in Hinduism, Jainism, and Sikhism. Typically observed in October or November, this vibrant and joyous holiday spans five days, illuminating homes and streets with lamps, candles, and fireworks. Diwali symbolizes the triumph of light over darkness and good over evil, with families coming together to share feasts, exchange gifts, and engage in religious ceremonies that foster a sense of unity, positivity, and spiritual renewal.

Messages

V1. Radiant Diwali Blessings: May Your Life Be Illuminated with Joy (#076)

As the festival of lights envelops us in its warm embrace, I extend heartfelt wishes for a Diwali filled with brilliance, joy, and prosperity. May the glow of diyas illuminate your path, dispelling darkness and bringing forth the radiant essence of happiness. May this auspicious occasion mark the beginning of a year filled with love, success, and the fulfillment of your deepest aspirations.

V2. A Symphony of Lights and Laughter: Diwali Greetings for You and Yours (#077)

On this joyous occasion of Diwali, may the melodious laughter of loved ones harmonize with the vibrant lights adorning your home. May the sweet melodies of celebration resonate through every corner of your life, filling each moment with positivity and warmth. Wishing you a Diwali brimming with togetherness, prosperity, and the boundless joy that comes from sharing this festival of lights with those who matter most.

V3. Sparkling Diwali Delights: May Your Days Be as Bright as the Fireworks (#078)

As the night sky explodes in a kaleidoscope of colors, your Diwali may be just as vibrant and joyful. May the fireworks sparkle reflect the brilliance of your dreams and aspirations, filling your days with excitement and success. This Diwali, may you be surrounded by the warmth of loved ones and the dazzling glow of prosperity, creating bright memories throughout the coming year.

V4. Luminous Diwali Wishes: May the Glow of Traditions Illuminate Your Heart (#079)

Embracing the richness of our cultural heritage, may this Diwali immerse you in the timeless traditions that bind us together. May the glow of diyas symbolize the triumph of light over darkness in your life, bringing forth a sense of peace, harmony, and spiritual enlightenment. I wish you a Diwali filled with the luminosity of love, familial bonds, and the timeless beauty of our shared customs.

V5. Divine Diwali Harmony: May the Goddess Lakshmi Bless Your Abode (#080)

On this sacred festival of Diwali, may the divine presence of Goddess Lakshmi grace your home with prosperity and abundance. May the traditional rituals of this auspicious day strengthen the bonds of family and community, creating an atmosphere of love and togetherness. May the lamp of knowledge dispel the shadows of ignorance, paving the way for a brighter and more enlightened future. Wishing you and your family a Diwali filled with divine blessings and the richness of spiritual fulfillment

Christmas

Christmas, observed on December 25th, is one of the most widely celebrated holidays globally. It holds significant cultural and religious importance, commemorating the birth of Jesus Christ. The festivities include decorating homes with lights and ornaments, exchanging gifts, attending church services, and sharing festive meals with family and friends. Christmas embodies the spirit of joy, love, and generosity, emphasizing the importance of kindness and compassion during the holiday season.

Messages

V1. Wishing You a Cozy Christmas Full of Joy and Laughter (#081)

As the snowflakes gently blanket the world outside, may the warmth of the holiday season fill your home with joy and laughter. May this Christmas be a time of togetherness, surrounded by loved ones, creating cherished memories that last a lifetime. Here's to a cozy and heartwarming holiday season!

V2. Sending Love and Peace Your Way this Christmas (#082)

In the spirit of love and peace, may this Christmas bring you moments of serenity and the comfort of being surrounded by those who matter most. May the twinkling lights and festive decorations illuminate your heart, filling it with the magic of the season. Wishing you a Christmas filled with love, joy, and tranquility.

V3. A Season of Blessings and Gratitude (#083)

As we gather with family and friends this Christmas, let's take a moment to appreciate the blessings that have graced our lives. May the spirit of gratitude shine brightly in our hearts, and may this holiday season bring you an abundance of joy, peace, and moments to be thankful for. Merry Christmas!

V4. May Your Christmas be Merry and Bright (#084)

With each twinkling light and the sound of familiar carols, may your Christmas be merry and bright. May the festive decorations and the warmth of loved ones create a magical atmosphere, turning every moment into a treasured memory. Here's to a joyous Christmas filled with laughter, love, and the simple pleasures that make the season special.

V5. Wishing You the Gift of Time and Togetherness (#085)

In the midst of the holiday hustle and bustle, may you find the true gifts of Christmas – time and togetherness. May this season be a reminder to cherish the moments with loved ones, creating bonds that withstand the test of time. Wishing you a Christmas filled with the warmth of shared smiles, the comfort of companionship, and the joy that comes from being surrounded by those who matter most.

Eid al-Fitr

Eid al-Fitr, often referred to as the "Festival of Breaking the Fast," marks the end of Ramadan, the Islamic holy month of fasting. Celebrated with prayers, feasts, and social gatherings, this joyous occasion signifies the accomplishment of spiritual discipline and the importance of compassion and charity towards others, especially those in need. Families come together to share meals, exchange gifts, and express gratitude for the blessings received during Ramadan.

Messages

V1. Wishing You Joy and Prosperity (#086)

As the holy month of Ramadan bids us farewell, may the divine blessings of Eid al-Fitr fill your life with joy, prosperity, and peace. May this special day top your efforts, bringing happiness to your heart and those around you.

V2. Eid Mubarak to You and Your Family (#087)

On this joyous occasion of Eid al-Fitr, may your home be filled with the warmth of love, the echoes of laughter, and the aroma of delicious feasts. May the bonds of family and friendship be strengthened, and may your days ahead be adorned with blessings.

V3. Gratitude and Celebration (#088)

As the crescent moon graces the sky, signaling the end of Ramadan, let us express gratitude for the month of reflection, self-discipline, and spiritual growth. May your Eid be a celebration of accomplishments and the beginning of a new chapter filled with peace, love, and understanding.

V4. Wishing You a Peaceful Reflection (#089)

As we bid farewell to Ramadan, may the spirit of Eid al-Fitr bring you moments of peaceful reflection and gratitude. May your heart be filled with the joy of sharing, the warmth of family, and the serenity of a renewed connection to your faith.

V5. Eid Greetings of Hope (#090)

I extend heartfelt Eid Mubarak wishes to you and your loved ones on this auspicious occasion. May the divine blessings of Eid al-Fitr inspire hope in your heart, illuminate your path, and fill your life with abundant joy, love, and kindness.

Thanksgiving

Thanksgiving is celebrated on the fourth Thursday of November in the United States. It is a time for expressing gratitude and coming together with family and friends. Traditionally rooted in a harvest festival, this holiday is marked by a festive meal, often featuring a roasted turkey, stuffing, and pumpkin pie. Beyond the culinary delights, Thanksgiving encourages reflection on the year's blessings and the importance of gratitude for the relationships and abundance in one's life.

Messages

V1. Expressing Gratitude for Togetherness (#091)

Happy Thanksgiving! On this special day, I want to express my deepest gratitude for the warmth and togetherness we share as a family. May our time together be filled with laughter, love, and the joy of creating lasting memories. Wishing you a Thanksgiving overflowing with blessings.

V2. A Heartfelt Thank You for Friendship (#092)

This Thanksgiving, I want to take a moment to thank you for being such a cherished friend. Your friendship has added a special flavor to my life, much like the spices in a Thanksgiving feast. May our bond continue to grow, and may your day be as wonderful as the memories we've created together.

V3. Grateful for the Simple Joys (#093)

As we gather around the table this Thanksgiving, let's take a moment to appreciate the simple joys that make life beautiful – the warmth of family, the comfort of good food, and the love surrounding us. Gratitude fills my heart today, and I'm thankful for the blessings that brighten each day.

V4. Appreciating the Blessings of the Year (#094)

This Thanksgiving, I find myself reflecting on the blessings that have graced my life throughout the year. From triumphs to challenges, each moment has shaped my journey. I'm thankful for the lessons learned, the growth achieved, and the unwavering support of loved ones. May your Thanksgiving be as abundant as the blessings in your life.

V5. Gratitude for the Journey (#095)

As we come together to celebrate Thanksgiving, let's take a moment to reflect on the journey we've traveled this year. There is much to be grateful for through highs and lows, twists and turns. I'm thankful for the strength that has carried us through, the love that binds us, and the shared moments that make life extraordinary. Wishing you a Thanksgiving filled with appreciation and joy.

Chinese New Year

Chinese New Year, also known as the Spring Festival, is a vibrant celebration in Chinese culture that marks the beginning of the lunar new year. This festive period lasts for 15 days, including dragon and lion dances, elaborate parades, and the iconic red decorations symbolizing good luck and prosperity. Families gather for reunion dinners, exchange red envelopes with money, and engage in customs believed to usher in luck, happiness, and prosperity for the coming year.

Messages

V1. Wishing You Abundance and Prosperity in the Year of the Ox (#096)

As we welcome the Year of the Ox, may your life be filled with boundless joy, prosperity, and good fortune. May the sturdy and hardworking nature of the Ox bring you success in all your endeavors. Here's to a year of growth, happiness, and fulfillment. Gong Xi Fa Cai!

V2. May the Dragon of Good Luck Smile Upon You (#097)

Sending warm wishes your way as we step into the Chinese New Year. May the mythical dragon of good luck and fortune bless your path, guiding you toward success and happiness. Embrace the coming Year with open arms, and may it bring you and your loved ones endless blessings. Xin Nian Kuai Le!

V3. A Year of Renewed Hope and Harmony (#098)

As the Chinese New Year unfolds, may it bring your life a sense of renewal and hope. May the melodies of joy and laughter fill your days, and may the Year of the Rat bring harmony to your relationships. Wishing you a year of peace, love, and endless possibilities. Gong Xi Fa Cai!

V4. Blossoming Happiness in the Year of the Blossom (#099)

In this Year of the Blossom, may your life bloom with happiness and prosperity. May the delicate petals of good health and success surround you, and may each day bring you closer to your dreams. Here's to a year of growth, joy, and vibrant experiences. Xin Nian Kuai Le!

V5. Prosperous Beginnings in the Year of the Tiger (#100)

As the Year of the Tiger roars in, may it bring forth courage, strength, and prosperity into your life. May you stride into new beginnings with confidence, and may the tiger's resilience inspire you to overcome any challenges that come your way. Wishing you a year filled with achievements, good health, and happiness. Gong Xi Fa Cai!

Bastille Day

Bastille Day, observed on July 14th, is France's National Day, commemorating the storming of the Bastille prison during the French Revolution. This significant holiday symbolizes the triumph of liberty, equality, and fraternity. Celebrations include grand parades along the Champs-Élysées, spectacular fireworks displays, and communal gatherings featuring French cuisine and traditional music. Bastille Day is a powerful reminder of the pursuit of freedom and the enduring spirit of the French Republic.

Messages

V1. *Celebrating Freedom* (#101)

May the spirit of liberty and equality fill your heart with joy on this Bastille Day. Wishing you a day filled with celebration and a reminder of the importance of standing united for freedom.

V2. *Joyeux 14 Juillet!* (#102)

As the French tricolor waves high, let's celebrate the ideals of Bastille Day – liberty, equality, and fraternity. May your day be filled with joy, laughter, and a sense of camaraderie with friends and family.

V3. *A Toast to Independence* (#103)

Cheers to the spirit of Bastille Day! May your day be filled with the joy of freedom, the warmth of friendship, and the taste of delicious French cuisine. Here's to celebrating the values that make us truly free.

V4. *Wishing You Revolutionary Happiness* (#104)

On this Bastille Day, let the revolutionary spirit inspire you to break free from any limitations. May your day be filled with joy, laughter, and the pursuit of your freedom.

V5. Vive la Liberté! (#105)

Happy Bastille Day! May the echoes of the French Revolution remind us all of the importance of freedom and the enduring power of unity. Here's to a day filled with pride, joy, and a celebration of the principles that make us truly free.

Halloween

Halloween, celebrated on October 31st, is a lively and playful festival with roots in Celtic and Christian traditions. Known for costumes, trick-or-treating, and spooky decorations, Halloween embraces the spirit of mystery and imagination. It's a time for both children and adults to indulge in creative costumes, share treats, and immerse themselves in the whimsical and eerie atmosphere of the season.

Messages

- Wishing you a spooktacular Halloween filled with treats that are sweeter than any trick! May your night be full of laughter, costumes, and the thrill of the haunted unknown. Happy Halloween!

- As the shadows lengthen and the moonlight dances, may your Halloween be filled with spooky delights and ghostly surprises. Here's to a night of frightful fun and sweet memories. Have a hair-raising Halloween!

- On this eerie night, may the pumpkins glow with an otherworldly light, the costumes bring smiles, and the candy flow in abundance. May your Halloween be enchanting and your heart be light. Happy Haunting!

- I wish you a Halloween brimming with spooky surprises and bewitching moments! May your night be filled with ghouls, ghosts, and goblins that bring more laughter than scares. Enjoy the thrills and chills of this magical night. Happy Halloween!

- May your Halloween be a cauldron of fun, bubbling with laughter and brimming with treats. From creepy crawlies to friendly spooks, may your night be filled with just the right amount of fright and a whole lot of delight. Happy Halloween!

Labor Day

Labor Day, celebrated on the first Monday of September in the United States, honors the contributions of workers and the labor movement. It's a day of rest and appreciation for the achievements of workers in various fields. Parades, picnics, and community events are common, reflecting the social and economic achievements of the labor force.

Messages

V1. Celebrating Your Hard Work (#106)

On this Labor Day, take a moment to recognize and celebrate your dedication and hard work. Your commitment to excellence not only benefits you but contributes to the strength of our entire community. May your efforts be acknowledged and appreciated today and every day.

V2. A Day to Relax and Reflect (#107)

As we commemorate Labor Day, I hope you find some well-deserved rest and reflection. Your tireless efforts contribute to the prosperity of our nation. Take this day to unwind, recharge, and revel in the fruits of your labor. Happy Labor Day!

V3. Honoring Your Work Ethic (#108)

Today is a day dedicated to honoring the incredible work ethic that you and countless others bring to the table every day. Your commitment and perseverance significantly impact our community and the world. May this Labor Day bring you a moment of well-earned relaxation and appreciation.

V4. Cheers to Your Dedication (#109)

Happy Labor Day! Your unwavering dedication to your work is truly commendable. Today, let's raise a toast to your efforts that contribute to the growth and prosperity of our society. May you take a break, enjoy the day, and know your hard work is valued and celebrated.

V5. Reflecting on Your Contributions (#110)

On this Labor Day, I want to express my gratitude for the dedication and contributions you make day in and day out. Your hard work not only propels your personal growth but also plays a crucial role in shaping the success of our community. May you take a moment to reflect on your accomplishments and enjoy a well-deserved break. Happy Labor Day!

International Women's Day

International Women's Day, observed on March 8th globally, celebrates the achievements of women and advocates for gender equality. The day highlights women's social, economic, cultural, and political accomplishments while raising awareness about their ongoing challenges. Various events, discussions, and initiatives take place to promote gender equity and women's rights.

Messages

V1. Celebrating Strength and Grace (#111)

Happy International Women's Day! Today, we honor the incredible strength and grace that women bring to the world. May you continue to inspire and empower those around you, making every day brighter. Here's to the remarkable women who shape our lives and our future.

V2. Acknowledging Resilience and Courage (#112)

On this International Women's Day, let's celebrate the resilience and courage of women everywhere. Your strength in facing challenges head-on and your unwavering determination inspire us all. Wishing you a day filled with recognition and appreciation for the incredible force you are.

V3. Empowering Voices, Inspiring Change (#113)

Happy International Women's Day! Today, we celebrate the power of your voice and its impact on shaping a more inclusive world. Your courage to speak up, inspire change, and champion equality is truly remarkable. May your journey be filled with continued strength and success.

V4. Championing Equality and Diversity (#114)

On International Women's Day, we stand united in the pursuit of equality and diversity. Your contribution to fostering an inclusive world is invaluable. May you be surrounded by love, support, and recognition today and always. Here's to breaking barriers and building a more equitable future together.

V5. Honoring Compassion and Empathy (#115)

Happy International Women's Day! Today, we celebrate the compassion and empathy that women bring to the table. Your ability to uplift others, nurture kindness, and create positive change is truly remarkable. May your day be filled with appreciation for the love and warmth you share with the world.

National Independence Day (Various Countries)

National Independence Day is celebrated in numerous countries worldwide, marking the day they gained independence from colonial rule or foreign domination. The celebrations often include patriotic displays, flag-hoisting ceremonies, parades, and cultural events. Examples include the Fourth of July in the United States, Bastille Day in France, and India's Independence Day.

Messages

V1. Celebrating Freedom Together (#116)

On this National Independence Day, let's unite in the spirit of freedom that binds us as a nation. May the colors of our flag inspire us to cherish the liberty we enjoy and work towards a brighter future for generations to come. Happy Independence Day!

V2. A Day of Pride and Gratitude (#117)

As we hoist our flag high and embrace the joyous festivities, let's take a moment to express gratitude to all those who fought for our freedom. May this Independence Day fill our hearts with pride for our nation and appreciation for the sacrifices that made this day possible.

V3. United We Stand, Stronger Than Ever (#118)

Happy Independence Day! Today, let's celebrate the unity that defines our nation. Together, we are stronger, and as we commemorate this day, let's reaffirm our commitment to working hand in hand for the prosperity and progress of our beloved country.

V4. *A Journey of Resilience and Hope* (#119)

On this National Independence Day, let's reflect on our nation's journey – a story of resilience, determination, and hope. As we mark this day, may it inspire us to face the challenges ahead with the same spirit that brought us freedom. Wishing everyone a day filled with pride and joy.

V5. *Freedom's Legacy, Tomorrow's Promise* (#120)

Happy Independence Day! Today, let's honor the legacy of freedom and reflect on the responsibility it bestows upon us. May we, as citizens, contribute to the progress and prosperity of our nation, ensuring that the promise of tomorrow is brighter and more inclusive for all.

SYMPATHY

In life, we inevitably encounter moments of sorrow and loss that prompt us to extend a hand of comfort and understanding. Expressing sympathy is an essential aspect of human connection, a gesture that acknowledges the pain others are going through and conveys our genuine care and support.

Wishing someone sympathy is more than just offering a few consoling words; it is a fundamental expression of empathy. It signifies understanding the emotional turbulence that grief brings and acknowledging the depth of someone's sorrow. In these moments, simplicity becomes a powerful tool. A genuine, straightforward message can provide solace and reassurance that the grieving individual is not alone in their pain.

When crafting sympathy wishes, being sincere and avoiding unnecessary complexities is crucial. Simple words, chosen with care, have the ability to transcend linguistic barriers and speak directly to the heart. A heartfelt "I'm sorry for your loss" or "My thoughts are with you during this difficult time" can offer comfort beyond elaborate expressions.

The simplicity of sympathy wishes also lies in the acknowledgment of the unknown. Grief is a unique journey for each individual, and it's impossible to comprehend the depth of someone else's sorrow fully. Simple wishes recognize this truth, offering support without presuming understanding the intricacies of another person's pain. This humility in expression creates a space for the grieving person to navigate their emotions at their own pace.

Moreover, the simplicity of sympathy wishes is a universal language of compassion. Regardless of cultural or linguistic differences, a genuine expression of sorrow transcends barriers and fosters a connection between individuals. In times of grief, the simplicity of heartfelt words becomes a bridge, linking hearts and fostering a sense of shared humanity.

Sympathy wishes are not limited to specific forms of communication. Whether conveyed through a handwritten note, a thoughtful email, or a heartfelt message, the simplicity of the sentiment remains constant. In today's interconnected world, a simple text message or a virtual card can carry as much weight as a traditional condolence letter, emphasizing that the essence of sympathy lies in the sincerity of the sentiment, not the medium through which it is conveyed.

In conclusion, the act of wishing someone sympathy is a testament to our shared humanity. Its simplicity speaks volumes about our capacity for compassion, understanding, and the willingness to stand alongside others during their moments of profound sorrow. By embracing the simplicity of sympathy wishes, we honor the strength of human connection and demonstrate that, even in the face of loss, simple expressions of empathy can provide a comforting balm for the wounded soul.

Loss of a Loved One

Losing a loved one is an incredibly challenging and emotionally overwhelming experience. It refers to the profound sorrow and grief one feels when someone close—a family member, friend, or significant other—passes away. The emotions associated with this loss can be complex, ranging from deep sadness and pain to a sense of emptiness or disbelief.

People experiencing the loss of a loved one often go through a grieving process, which is unique to each individual. The grieving process may involve various stages, such as denial, anger, bargaining, depression, and acceptance, though not everyone experiences them in the same order or intensity. It's important to recognize that grief is a natural response to loss, and individuals may need time and support to navigate through their emotions.

During such difficult times, offering sympathy to someone who has lost a loved one involves expressing condolences, acknowledging the pain they are going through, and offering support. Simple gestures like sending a sympathy card, attending a memorial service, or offering a listening ear can comfort those grieving. It's essential to be sensitive to their needs and allow them to grieve in their own way and time, understanding that healing is a gradual process.

Loss of a loved one is a universal human experience, and while the pain may never fully subside, with time and support, individuals can learn to cope with the loss and find ways to honor and remember the departed loved one.

Messages

VI. (#121)

Dear [Name],

I'm deeply saddened to hear about the passing of your [relationship of the departed]. Please accept my heartfelt condolences during this incredibly difficult time. [Name of the departed] was an extraordinary person, and I feel fortunate to have known them. Their memory will forever hold a special place in our hearts, and I hope you find solace in the cherished moments you shared. My thoughts and prayers are with you and your family.

With deepest sympathy,

[Your Name]

V2. (#122)

Dear [Name],

I was truly sorry to learn about the loss of your [relationship of the departed]. The news brought great sadness, and I can't imagine the pain you're going through. [Name of the departed] was a remarkable individual, and their kindness touched the lives of everyone around them. Please know that I am here for you during this challenging time. May you find strength in the love and support of friends and family.

Sending you my sincere condolences,

[Your Name]

V3. (#123)

Dear [Name],

I want to extend my deepest sympathy to you and your family as you navigate through the loss of your [relationship of the departed]. Losing someone we care about is never easy, and words can't adequately express the sorrow I feel for you. [Name of the departed] will be remembered for [his/her] warmth, laughter, and the positive impact [he/she] had on everyone fortunate enough to know [him/her]. My thoughts and prayers are with you during this trying time.

With heartfelt condolences,

[Your Name]

V4. (#124)

Dear [Name],

I was saddened to hear about the passing of your [relationship of the departed]. Please accept my sincere condolences as you mourn the loss of such a beloved soul. [Name of the departed] left an indelible mark on the lives [he/she] touched, and [his/her] memory will forever be a source of inspiration. During this time of grief, I hope you find strength in the love and memories you shared.

Wishing you peace and comfort,

[Your Name]

V5. (#125)

Dear [Name],

It is with a heavy heart that I extend my deepest condolences on the passing of your [relationship of the departed]. [Name of the departed] was a remarkable person who brought so much joy and positivity into the lives of those around [him/her]. In this difficult time, may you find solace in the beautiful memories you shared and the love surrounding you. My thoughts are with you, and I am here to offer support in any way you may need.

With sympathy,

[Your Name]

Illness or Health Struggles

When someone is going through illness or health struggles, it means that they are dealing with physical or mental health challenges that are impacting their well-being. This can include a wide range of conditions, from temporary illnesses like the flu to chronic health issues such as diabetes or mental health disorders like anxiety or depression.

In the context of sending a sympathy message for illness or health struggles, it usually refers to expressing empathy and support for someone facing these challenges. This might involve undergoing medical treatments, coping with pain or discomfort, and dealing with the emotional and psychological toll that health issues can bring.

A sympathetic message in this context would convey understanding, care, and encouragement. It's a way of letting the person know you acknowledge their struggles, offer support, and wish them strength and healing. This type of message aims to provide comfort and reassurance during a difficult time, emphasizing the importance of emotional support and solidarity when facing health-related challenges.

Messages

V1. Message of Support for a Friend Undergoing Treatment (#126)

Hey [Friend's Name], I heard about your recent health challenges, and I want you to know that you're in my thoughts every day. Your strength and resilience are truly inspiring. Sending lots of positive vibes your way, and I'm here for you no matter what you need. Wishing you a smooth journey through treatment and a speedy recovery.

V2. Encouragement for a Family Member Facing Surgery (#127)

Dearest [Family Member's Name], as you face this upcoming surgery, know that our entire family is rallying behind you. Your courage is unmatched, and we believe in your ability to conquer whatever comes your way. Sending you all the love and strength in the world. Here's to a successful surgery and a swift recovery. We're here for you every step of the way.

V3. Heartfelt Wishes for a Colleague Battling Health Issues (#128)

Dear [Colleague's Name], learning about your health struggles was tough news for all of us at work. Your dedication and hard work have always been an inspiration to the team. Take all the time you need to focus on your health and don't hesitate to reach out if you need anything. I wish you a steady recovery and look forward to seeing you back in the office when you're ready.

V4. Warm Thoughts for a Neighbor Facing a Long-term Health Journey (#129)

Hi [Neighbor's Name], I recently heard about your health journey, and I want you to know that you're not alone. Your strength is admirable, and your positivity is contagious. If there's anything I can do to make your days a bit brighter, please don't hesitate to ask. Sending healing thoughts your way and hoping for better days ahead.

V5. Personalized Message for a Friend Dealing with Chronic Illness (#130)

To my dear friend [Friend's Name], I've seen the challenges you've faced with your chronic illness, and your resilience never ceases to amaze me. Your positive spirit in the face of adversity is truly commendable. Remember that you have a support system that cares deeply about you. I'm here to lend an ear or a helping hand whenever you need it. I wish you strength, comfort, and brighter days ahead.

Job Loss or Financial Strain

Job Loss or Financial Strain is when an individual experiences a loss of employment or faces significant financial difficulties. This can be a challenging and stressful time, impacting various aspects of a person's life. Several factors can contribute to job loss or financial strain, including economic downturns, company closures, personal health issues, or unforeseen circumstances.

Common Aspects of Job Loss or Financial Strain

Emotional Impact: Losing a job can lead to a range of emotions, including shock, disbelief, frustration, and even a sense of identity loss. The uncertainty of the future and financial instability can add to the emotional burden.

Financial Instability: Job loss often results in a sudden reduction or loss of income, leading to financial strain. Individuals may struggle to meet daily expenses, pay bills, or cover essential needs, causing stress and anxiety.

Career Transition: Job loss can also trigger a period of career transition. Individuals may need to reassess their skills, update their resumes, and explore new job opportunities, which can be both challenging and time-consuming.

Impact on Personal Life: Financial strain can affect personal relationships and family dynamics. The stress of economic difficulties may lead to strained relationships, communication breakdowns, and challenges in maintaining a healthy work-life balance.

Health and Well-being: The emotional and financial toll of job loss or financial strain can impact a person's mental and physical well-being. Stress-related health issues may arise, highlighting the importance of seeking support and maintaining overall health during this period.

Seeking Support: During times of job loss or financial strain, individuals may benefit from seeking support from friends, family, or professional networks. Support can come in the form of emotional encouragement, advice on job searching, or assistance in managing finances.

Navigating job loss or financial strain is undoubtedly challenging, but with support, resilience, and proactive efforts, individuals can overcome these difficulties and work towards rebuilding their professional and financial stability.

Messages

V1. *Message of Support for Job Loss* (#131)

I just heard about your job loss, and I want you to know that I'm here for you. Losing a job can be incredibly challenging, but please remember that your worth is not defined by your job title. Take the time you need to process; when you're ready, I'm here to support you in any way I can. You have valuable skills, and I believe in your resilience to navigate through this tough period. I am sending positive thoughts your way.

V2. *Condolences and Encouragement* (#132)

I was saddened to hear about your job loss. Please accept my deepest condolences during this difficult time. I know that it's not easy, but I want you to remember that you're not alone in this journey. You have a network of friends and family who care about you. Take the time you need to heal, and when you're ready, there are opportunities waiting for someone as capable and dedicated as you. Wishing you strength and brighter days ahead.

V3. Offering a Helping Hand (#133)

I heard the news about your job and want you to know I'm here for you. If there's anything I can do to support you during this challenging time, whether it's helping with your resume, providing job leads, or just being a listening ear, please don't hesitate to reach out. Your skills are valuable, and I am confident you will find new opportunities. Take a deep breath, and remember that this setback is temporary. Better days are ahead.

V4. Words of Comfort and Encouragement (#134)

I know that losing your job is not easy to go through, and I'm here to offer my support in any way you need. It's okay to feel a mix of emotions right now, but please know that this setback doesn't define your future. You have talents and strengths that will open doors to new opportunities. Take the time to take care of yourself, and when you're ready, I'm here to help you navigate the path forward. You've got this.

V5. Personalized Encouragement for Financial Strain (#135)

I understand that facing financial strain can be incredibly stressful. Please know that you're not alone, and there's no shame in seeking support. If you need assistance in budgeting, exploring financial resources, or just someone to talk to, I'm here for you. Remember that your worth goes beyond your financial situation, and you can overcome these challenges with resilience and determination. Lean on your support system, and we'll find a way through together. Take care.

Relationship Breakup or Divorce

A relationship breakup or divorce refers to the formal or informal dissolution of a romantic or marital relationship between two individuals. It is a process in which a couple decides to end their union, often involving legal procedures in the case of divorce. The reasons for a breakup or divorce can vary widely, ranging from irreconcilable differences and communication issues to more serious matters like infidelity or incompatible life goals.

This emotional and often challenging event can significantly impact the lives of those involved, including the couple, their families, and sometimes even close friends. The decision to end a relationship is rarely made lightly and can stem from a culmination of issues that make it difficult for individuals to sustain a healthy and fulfilling connection.

The breakup or divorce process typically involves several stages, including the decision to separate, legal proceedings (if applicable), emotional adjustment, and, ideally, personal growth. Both parties may experience a range of emotions, such as grief, sadness, anger, and relief, as they navigate the complexities of untangling their lives from each other.

Support from friends, family, or mental health professionals can be crucial during this time to help individuals cope with emotional challenges and build resilience. It's important for those going through a breakup or divorce to allow themselves the time and space to heal, reflect on the experience, and gradually move forward with their lives.

While the end of a relationship is undoubtedly difficult, it can also mark the beginning of new opportunities for personal growth, self-discovery, and, eventually, the possibility of finding a healthier and more compatible connection in the future.

Messages

VI. Empathy and Support (#136)

I heard about your recent breakup, and I just wanted to let you know that I'm here for you. Breakups are never easy, and it's okay to feel a mix of emotions.

Take your time to heal, and know that you're not alone. If you need someone to talk to or a shoulder to lean on, I'm just a call away.

V2. Strength and Resilience (#137)

I know this is a tough time for you, and I want you to know that your strength in facing this breakup is admirable. It's okay to grieve the end of a relationship. As you navigate through the healing process, remember that you have the resilience within you to come out stronger. Take each day at your own pace, and I'm here to support you in any way you need.

V3. Navigating Change (#138)

Change is never easy, especially when it comes to matters of the heart. I want you to know that I am here to support you through this period of transition. Whether it's lending a listening ear or just being there for you, I'm committed to helping you navigate through this change. You are not alone, and you will emerge from this stronger than ever.

V4. Encouragement for the Future (#139)

While endings can be painful, they also mark the beginning of new chapters. As you navigate through this breakup, I want to encourage you to focus on self-discovery and personal growth. Use this time to rediscover what brings you joy and fulfillment. The future holds new opportunities for happiness, and I believe in your ability to create a positive and fulfilling life ahead.

V5. Taking Time for Healing (#140)

I understand that going through a breakup is an incredibly challenging experience. It's okay to take the time you need to heal and reflect. Your emotions are valid, and there's no rush in moving forward. Surround yourself with supportive friends and activities that bring you comfort. Remember, healing is a process, and I'm here to support you every step of the way.

Feeling Overwhelmed or Stressed

Feeling overwhelmed or stressed refers to a state of emotional and mental strain resulting from various factors that exceed an individual's ability to cope. It's a common human experience triggered by a variety of situations, such as excessive workloads, personal challenges, unexpected events, or a combination of stressors.

When someone expresses that they are feeling overwhelmed or stressed, it often implies that they are struggling to manage the demands placed on them. This could manifest in a range of emotions, including anxiety, frustration, and a sense of being unable to cope with the pressures in their life. The feeling may be both mental and physical, impacting their thoughts, emotions, and even their physical well-being.

Common sources of stress or overwhelm include work-related pressures, relationship issues, financial concerns, health challenges, or a combination of these factors. Each person's threshold for handling stress is different, and what may be manageable for one individual can become overwhelming for another.

Offering support to someone experiencing stress involves empathetic listening, understanding their feelings, and providing reassurance. Encouraging them to seek professional help if needed, practicing self-care, and identifying healthy coping mechanisms are essential steps toward managing stress and regaining a sense of balance and well-being. Remembering that it's okay to ask for help and that support is available can be crucial in navigating through these challenging emotions.

Messages

V1. (#141)

I can see that things have been really tough for you lately, and I just want you to know that I'm here for you. Life can throw us curveballs, and it's okay to feel overwhelmed. Remember, you don't have to face it all alone. If you need to talk or if there's anything I can do to lighten your load, just let me know. You're not alone in this; together, we'll find a way through.

V2. (#142)

I've noticed that you've been carrying a heavy burden lately, and I want you to know that it's okay to feel stressed. Life can be challenging, but it's important to recognize when you need support. I'm here to lend an understanding ear and to help in any way I can. You're not alone in this, and your well-being matters. Take a deep breath, and let's navigate through this together.

V3. (#143)

I've sensed that you've been under a lot of pressure, and I just want to remind you that it's okay to feel overwhelmed. You don't have to have everything figured out. If you need a break, someone to talk to, or even just a moment of quiet, I'm here for you. Your feelings are valid, and taking care of yourself is important. Let's work through this together, one step at a time.

V4. (#144)

Life can be incredibly demanding, and it seems like you're going through a challenging time. I want you to know that it's okay to feel stressed, and you don't have to carry the weight alone. If you need someone to share the load with, I'm here. Whether it's a conversation, a helping hand, or simply a moment of support, count on me to be there. We'll face these challenges together, and I believe brighter days are ahead.

V5. (#145)

I've noticed that the pressures of life are taking a toll on you, and I just want to express my concern and support. Feeling overwhelmed is a common experience, but it's crucial to reach out when you need help. I'm here for you, not only to share the load but to navigate through the stress together. Your well-being matters, and I believe that with the right support, we can find a way to ease the burden you're carrying. You're not alone in this journey.

CONCLUSION

As we reach the end of **"The Perfect Words For Every Special Occasion,"** I hope this journey through the art of crafting meaningful messages has been both enlightening and inspiring. In the vast landscape of human communication, our ability to convey sentiments and emotions through thoughtful words holds immeasurable power.

This guide has been crafted with the belief that every occasion, whether a joyous celebration or a challenging moment, is an opportunity to connect, uplift, and empathize with those we care about. Throughout the chapters, we've explored the nuances of crafting original and genuine messages, emphasizing the importance of knowing your recipient, infusing warmth, and expressing genuine emotion.

Whether it's celebrating birthdays, weddings, new homes, graduations, retirements, special holidays, or offering heartfelt condolences during times of sympathy, this guide has provided practical insights and examples to assist you in navigating the delicate art of words.

Remember, the right words have the ability to create lasting memories, strengthen relationships, and offer solace in times of need. By adding a personal touch, tailoring messages to individuals, and keeping your expressions positive and uplifting, you have the power to make your words resonate deeply with those who receive them.

May this guide serve as a constant companion in your journey of thoughtful communication. As you embark on crafting messages for various occasions, may your words be a source of joy, comfort, and connection. The canvas of life is painted with the strokes of our words, and with each carefully chosen sentiment, we contribute to the masterpiece of human connection.

I wish you a world filled with beautifully articulated thoughts and heartfelt expressions. May your words continue to weave the tapestry of meaningful relationships and shared moments. Thank you for exploring the art of thoughtful messages with me.